Stop
The Madness

How the Highly Sensitive Person Can Thrive in a Chaotic World

Johnnie M Urban
Strategic Interventionist
MNLP, Life Success & Business Coach
And A Highly Sensitive Person

Copyright 2015

All rights reserved

Stop The Pain, How The Highly Sensitive Person Can Thrive In The Chaotic World
Copyright 2015

This title is also available on Kindle
*Visit **www.WonderfulLifeLearning.com***

Request for information should be addressed to:
info@wonderfullifelearning.com

This addition:
ISBN-13: 978-1514200278

ISBN-10: 1514200279

All rights reserved. No part of this publication may be reproduced, stored, in a retrieval system, or transmitted in any form or by any means-electronic, mechanical, photocopy, recording, or any other- except for brief quotations in printed reviews, without the prior permission of the publisher.

Cover design and illustration: Kim Johnson
Edited by: Fiverr.com writerlisaz
Photography by: Michelle Fairless, www.michellefairless.com

Printed in the United States

Dedication

This book is dedicated to all the Highly Sensitive People who show us every day the beauty and passion of life.
As always my gratitude to God for all that is good.

Acknowledgements

I want to thank my friends and family for their loving support as I worked on this project.

I thank God, not first but always, for his truly unconditional love and the challenges He presents so that we may learn, grow, and love all His children, all the time. I have profound appreciation for His sending Jesus to provide a way back to Him.

I am also grateful for the teaching and influence of my dear friend, Tony Robbins, and his wife, Bonnie Pearl, as God uses them both to spark a new flame of hope within my heart and soul that life is what I make it. They taught me that we all have a choice to choose well.

To my husband, Michael, who every day sees the gifts that God has given to us and supports my dreams no matter how crazy they seem to him.

My deep gratitude to Kim Johnson, my coach and dear friend who knows me so well, inside and out. She is the one person in my life that sees all of me and loves me enough to have empathy and loves me even more to hold me to my greatness.

My gratefulness to Dr. Elaine Aron and Ted Zeff, Ph.D., for their insights, studies, and books about the Highly Sensitive Person. To bring the unknown into the light changes everything.

My appreciation to all the contributors, Karen Sully and Kathleen Rockney, for USANA. Dr. Corey King, my friend, Lynn Kay, Kathy Mulherin, and Chris Kussoff at my Egoscue clinic.

They all touch my heart deeply, for without their insights, this book would not have been as complete.

All the stories of my clients have either been used with permission or are a compilation of many people and experiences. These stories were carefully chosen so that you could see that you are not alone and perhaps learn from other Highly Sensitive People. I have been careful, however, to protect all confidential information my clients have shared with me. My clients become my teachers, and I thank them as well.

Always remember we are just three things;

What we are born with.
What we are taught.
And what we choose to do with it.

Table of Contents

CHAPTER ONE 8
- WHO IS DRIVING THE BUS? 8
- WHAT IS A HIGHLY SENSITIVE PERSON? 13
- THE TROUBLE WITH BEING AN HSP/HSS 17
- EMOTIONAL REGULATION 18
- 11 THINGS EVERYONE GETS WRONG ABOUT HIGHLY SENSITIVE PEOPLE 21
- A HIGHLY SENSITIVE ENTREPRENEUR? 26
- WHY HSP ARE DESIGNED FOR SELF-EMPLOYMENT 28
- WHAT EXACTLY IS NETWORK MARKETING? 30
- YOUR COMFORT ZONE IS YOUR BROKE ZONE! 31

CHAPTER TWO 36
- DEFINE YOUR ABILITIES 36
- 5 WAYS THAT CAN HELP HS PEOPLE MANAGE THEIR ABILITIES 39
- "ISN'T IT JUST FEMININE ENERGY?" 42
- THE SHADOW SIDE TO HIGH SENSITIVITY 48
- THE HIGHLY SENSITIVE PERSON IN A RELATIONSHIP 56
- 8 SURPRISING FACTS ABOUT HIGHLY SENSITIVE SPOUSES ... 59
- HSP AND 6 HUMAN NEEDS 66

CHAPTER THREE 77
- HOW TO EXIST IN THE CHAOTIC WORLD 77
- BAM, I FOUND IT 82
- REFRAMING 85
- THE IMPORTANCE OF NUTRITION AND WELLNESS 89
- MEETING DR. COREY KING 93
- RELAX, RESTORE, AND REVIVE YOUR MIND AND BODY 94
- USANA NUTRITIONAL PROGRAM 95
- EGOSCUE PAIN FREE CENTERS 100
- REAL SCIENCE, REAL RESULTS 105
- BE YOUR OWN HEALTH ADVOCATE 109

CHAPTER FOUR 112
- YOUR FAITH, GOD NEVER WASTES A PAIN 112
- DAILY EXERCISES ABOUT SPIRITUAL LIFE 114

PRAY DIFFERENTLY...117
JESUS CALLING 118
JOURNAL WRITING SYSTEM 120
LESS IS MORE 124
THE PEARL NECKLACE 126

CHAPTER FIVE...130

SOLUTIONS 130
POWERFUL QUESTIONS 131
MORNING ACTIVATION QUESTIONS 131
EVENING CALMING QUESTIONS..132
INNER OR OUTER ENERGY?...135
HSP TRAVELING..139
THE UNIQUE HSP 144
THE HSP TRIBE 147
SOURCES...148

Introduction

This book has been written for you by a Highly Sensitive Person who gets you.

I am going to share with you how you, a Highly Sensitive Person, can live and thrive in the chaotic, crisis driven world we are in so that you can be happy, successful, and at peace in the chaos.

Take note that throughout this book I will refer to the term Highly Sensitive Person as HSP.

Information that I have presented here is in no way meant to replace actual psychological therapy, professional counseling, or coaching. It is designed to help you understand the Highly Sensitive Person trait that you or someone you know may have that could be causing stress, overwhelm, and exhaustion in your life.

It is my intention, as a professionally trained and experienced coach, to guide you with information that may help you navigate the chaotic world. To provide you with understanding, support, guidance, and information that has helped me and other HSPs to live happy, peaceful, thriving lives.

Peace...
"It does not mean to be in a place where there is no noise, trouble, or hard work. It means to be in the midst of those things and still be calm in your heart."

When I was growing up, I distinctly remember hating it whenever I heard someone else complaining about and judging someone. I always needed to defend the underdog and tell the judgers to just let them be who they are. It became my motto, just let them BE!

Now I realize it's because when I heard or saw people treating others wrong, I felt it deeply within myself and I needed it to stop.

Learning to manage this "feeling deeply" trait of an HSP has been a roller coaster ride for me. I've heard a great deal of advice from a lot of well-meaning people that practically drove me crazy. I always felt like they were telling me there was something wrong with me and THEY had the magic method that would fix it.

Feeling deeply, for an HSP, is as natural as breathing air.

When feeling deeply is beautiful and expanding you will feel alive and authentic to your core.
When it is gut wrenching, torture, and exhausting is when we want the madness to stop.

I am here to tell you that you have a choice of doing what works best for you.

Yes, it will be the cause of crying while experiencing a beautiful song that moves you, or a work of art, or a flower in your garden. It will also cause you to stop an injustice, help someone get out of their pain, or build a successful business that employs people and contributes to the community.

If someone were to ask an HSP to stop feeling deeply as a way to protect themselves, then they are also asking them to give up a piece of who they are.

Will there be times that you will feel overwhelmed with emotion when it's not convenient? Absolutely! That is when you will need to use some useful techniques that I have included in later chapters of this book.

Of everything that you will read and learn here in this book and in your own research and personal experiences, there is one thing that's really important for you to know about being an HSP. We may fit into the description of being an HSP, but we are all uniquely different. As unique as our fingerprints. Even identical twins have their own unique fingerprints.

Using My HSP Traits And Abilities

Back when I was a child, I wished that there was someone I could have spoken to about this stuff. I was so confused, alone, and unsure about what I was experiencing in my life every moment of every day.

That is exactly why I have taken my coaching passion and skills into helping people like you that are still looking for the answers to your HSP challenges.

I tap into my HSP traits as an ability that makes me a unique coach for people like you.

I chose as the title of my book, **Stop The Madness**, because there are so many Highly Sensitive People out there in the world that are suffering from overwhelm, exhaustion, and the crazy-making of other people.

These are beautifully talented people that are hiding, not using their gifts and abilities because the very thought of possibly being overwhelmed is terrifying and exhausting.

Whoever You Are...

Why is it important for you to know about the traits and abilities of the Highly Sensitive Person?

How would you like to celebrate, proudly proclaim, stand tall, and be authentic about being a Highly Sensitive Person?

Celebrate Your Abilities. Honor Your traits. Thrive In A Chaotic World.

Here are a couple questions I have for you:

- What are you choosing?

- Are you giving or taking?

Highly Sensitive People are designed to be giving.

If we are not giving our love, joy, happiness, and heartfelt gratefulness, then we are only existing, not thriving. And because a Highly Sensitive Person is so attuned to what is working and not working, we will feel guilt and shame if we are not contributing.

Here in this book, you will learn what Highly Sensitive Person traits and abilities are and how they can be a challenge and a blessing.
You will learn how to transform your emotional and physical pain into a new, wonderful you that contributes to your relationships, community, and even the world.

You will be able to:

Stop The Madness
And Thrive In A Chaotic World

Any and all questions or comments about your learnings and experiences are welcome.

**You can always find me at
www.WonderfulLifeLearning.com.**

Included with the purchase of every book is a copy of a complimentary companion workbook **40 Days To Fulfillment - Where Are You Going To Be In 40 Days?**

All you have to do is email your receipt to; info@WonderfulLifeLearning@gmail.com
Subject line: workbook, and you will receive a link for your downloadable workbook.

Chapter One

Who is driving the Bus?

I was coaching a client the other day about how frustrated she was about what a difficult week she was having. Her day would start out good but then, no matter what she did, within hours she was a mess. She would get stuck in traffic, be late for work and appointments, and forget her lunch at home; her co-workers were mean, and her son was constantly texting with a problem. By two p.m., she was overwhelmed, exhausted, and ready to call it quits for the third day in a row.

At this point I was saying, "Thank God." If she had not had her terrible three days, then she wouldn't be ready to learn from it all. We got together just in time to stop the madness of her spiraling up and down.

Through our conversation, I was able to quickly gather from her enough information to determine that she was choosing helplessness to drive her bus.

The bus is a metaphor that I use for our life and how we operate in our waking hours, minutes, and even seconds. Yes, seconds, because you and I both know that decisions and change can be made in a heartbeat.

This single mom is smart, energetic, and strong. Sometimes those are great attributes and sometimes they are heavy weights to bear.

When an HSP is not allowing herself to be vulnerable and ask for help (see chapter about Shadows), then all those people around her have expectations about her. What can you expect, we trained them well, didn't we? Yet, when HSPs are tired from not enough sleep or proper nutrition or time to themselves, then you can only guess what could happen.

The shadow of "not allowing others to see you weak" takes over and is allowed to drive the bus of your life.
We all have a bus that holds all the parts of us, and the bus has to have a driver. From the moment we wake up in the morning to bedtime, the bus is humming along through our day taking us wherever we need to go.

My client was starting her day off with the "responsible" driver that quickly changed to "frustrated" driver when she arrived late for work. As an HSP, she did not want to feel shame for being late so she let the helpless injured "please don't hurt me" person drive the bus. When her coworkers and boss didn't feel sorry for her, she labeled them as being mean.
What came next was her son constantly interrupting her "wounded" driver with requests to rescue him from his problems.

She is torn between being a strong Mom to being a wounded HSP. A recipe for overwhelm and exhaustion.

Fortunately, we get to choose who is driving the bus at any given time. Sometimes it's not going to be easy but my hope is that with the information that I have provided in this book, you will begin to know that there is hope for you and anyone else that you know who is Highly Sensitive.

Journaling

You will notice that at the end of each section there is space for you to jot down or journal any thoughts or feelings as you experience them from the previous chapter. The journaling will be your first step to being a participant in your own rescue.

Journal
Who's driving your bus?

A Highly Sensitive Person Song

Who I Was Born To Be Lyrics
Susan Boyle
from I Dreamed A Dream

When I was a child
I could see the wind in the trees
And I heard a song in the breeze
It was there, singing out my name

But I am not a girl
I have known the taste of defeat
And I've finally grown to believe
It will all came around again

And though I may not know the answers
I can finally say I am free
And if the questions led me here
Then I am who I was born to be

And so here am I
Open arms and ready to stand
I've got the world in my hands
And it feels like my turn to fly

Though I may not know the answers
I can finally say I am free
And if the questions led me here
Then I am who I was born to be

When I was a child
There were flowers that bloomed in the night
Unafraid to take in the light
Unashamed to have braved the dark

Though I may not know the answers
I can finally say I am free
And if the questions led me here
Then I am who I was born to be
I am who I was born to be

***

What Is A Highly Sensitive Person?

Have you ever had moments in your life where you thought you were going crazy?

You feel that the world around you and the people in it are just so very different from you.

You feel like you don't belong in the group, at work, even your family.

That your family and friends just do not get you, and after being with them you are utterly exhausted.

You only have one really close friend, perhaps two, whom you fit with when you are together.
You almost don't have to say anything and just know what each other is feeling. Did you notice that I said feeling not thinking?

Have you ever looked at a piece of art so deeply that you began to feel yourself becoming one with it and at times you are fighting back tears of profound connection and joy?

The attributes of HSPs can be remembered as DOES:

Depth of processing
Over aroused (easily as compared to others)
Emotional reactivity and high empathy
Sensitivity to subtle stimuli

If the above sound true to you, you may be highly sensitive. The personality trait — which was first researched by Elaine N. Aron, Ph.D., in the early 1990s — is relatively common, with as many as one in five people possessing it. Aron, who has written multiple studies and books on high sensitivity, including *The Highly Sensitive Person*, also developed a self-test (which you can take here http://hsperson.com/test/highly-sensitive-test/).

The results will help to determine if you are a highly sensitive person.

Ted Zeff, Ph.D., author of *The Highly Sensitive Person's Survival Guide* and other books on highly sensitive people points out these traits of HSP:

- *They feel more deeply.*
- *They're more emotionally reactive.*
- *They're probably used to hearing, "Don't take things so personally" and "Why are you so sensitive?"*
- *They prefer to exercise solo.*
- *It takes longer for them to make decisions.*
- *They are more upset if they make a "bad" or "wrong" decision.*
- *They're extremely detail-oriented.*
- *Not all highly sensitive people are introverts.*
- *They work well in team environments.*
- *They're more prone to anxiety or depression (but only if they've had a lot of past negative experiences).*
- *That annoying sound is probably significantly more annoying to a highly sensitive person.*
- *Violent movies are the worst.*
- *They cry more easily.*
- *They have above-average manners.*
- *The effects of criticism are especially amplified in highly sensitive people.*
- *Cubicles = good. Open-office plans = bad.*

If all or some of the above describes you, then you have the traits of a highly sensitive person.

Like it or not, you were born with these traits and abilities and it has an impact on your life.

That impact is sometimes positive and mostly chaotic. The simple reason is because, according to research, we are only 20% of the total population. We are literally outnumbered.

Later on in this chapter I have provided the research plus how other countries view the HSP traits.

My HSS Discovery

I have to share something with you…

Just about two years ago, in early 2013, It came to my awareness that I too was an HSP.

Full disclosure: I almost completely rejected the whole idea. Yet, my personality fit into almost all the descriptions of what an HSP was all about.
Talk about total confusion.

Over the course of the process of learning exactly what this meant for me and my world, I discovered that what my mentors were teaching was not quite a fit.

Like I had just bought a new jacket that I loved yet every time I put it on and attempted to go about my life, it just didn't fit right.

I accepted and was relieved of what a huge piece of being highly sensitive meant, yet a piece was missing. I couldn't let it go, like a dog on a bone, I had to find out. I went back to Elaine Aron's Blog site, *The Comfort Zone*, and began reading until I found this one:

The Trouble With Being An HSP/HSS

From Elaine Aron:
"I have always used the analogy one HSP/HSS gave me, which was that she felt like she lived with one foot on the gas, one foot on the brake. But in fact, both parts are drivers, with human concerns and strategies for getting their way.
Hence HSP/HSSs more often feel like two people in a constant argument. And the HSS part often wins because in this culture, at least, the combination of curiosity, competitiveness (more typical of HSSs), and risk taking are all admired more than the HSP combination of traits. Hence the HSP part often feels it has less power and is more often dominated by the HSS part."

Now I know why I was feeling incomplete.

It was because I am a High Sensation Seeker (HSS). According to research, this is a subset of an HSP. About 30% of all HSP are HSS.

If you think you might be a HSS, you can take the HSS test here: http://hsperson.com/test/high-sensation-seeking-test/ .

What this meant for me was that I would search for and be active in new adventures in my life and business but then crash and burn when I bit off more than I could chew.

I learned to add prayer for discernment in my choices and learned to let go of regret for not doing what I wanted or committed to do.

Emotional Regulation

Elaine Aron writes in her blog that emotional regulation is important for an HSP and a HSS.

"A simplified definition of emotional regulation is to feel the right emotion for your long-term wellbeing, at the right time, and in the right intensity for you. HSPs, having so many strong and subtle emotions, must develop emotional regulation, especially early in life, but throughout life.

Because emotions are their tool, artists do not feel negative about negative emotions, another important part of emotional regulation. HSPs also need to accept whatever they feel rather than feel additional shame, fear, or anger about having the emotion. And if there IS shame about the feelings they feel, that they have the capacity to fly in the face of that shame and express their feelings anyway. This could be why many artists are often credited as "being so brave." Finally, often artists have learned they can tolerate strong emotions, also essential to emotional regulation. HSPs need to learn that confidence as well. We will survive this wave of feeling.

Since artists are often expressing emotions stirred up by love, they help us regulate the emotions specific to love as well, vicariously. In our first HSP study (published in 1997), we asked and found it to be true that HSPs report feeling love more intensely than others.

When we have fallen "head over heels" or lost someone we love, or been rejected or betrayed, poems and songs about the resulting feelings make us aware of how we feel, make us feel okay about feeling so intensely because we are not alone, and help us tolerate these tidal waves of emotion by finding out others also have them. (Although sometimes poems and songs also stir things up, so we need to know when to stop listening, too.)"

Journal
List what stirs your emotions...

11 Things Everyone Gets Wrong About Highly Sensitive People

This is a quick and to the point basic description of traits of an HSP. It is one of the first pieces of information that I found that accurately described why I felt that I was unique and different from non-HSPs. I have also found that this piece of information is useful when I need to explain to people exactly what being Highly Sensitive is.

The following was written by Dr. Elaine Aron and posted on her website on November 21st, 2014. You can go to her website http://hsperson.com/comfort-zone/ for more valuable articles and blog posts going way back to 2004.

"You're just too sensitive. Don't take things so personally."

In a culture that favors the powerful, sensitivity can be seen as a deficiency. Sensitive people can be perceived as delicate, quiet and aloof, but that doesn't mean sensitivity is a negative trait. Being a highly sensitive individual may be more useful than the common wisdom would have us believe, according to researcher and psychologist Elaine N. Aron, Ph.D. In fact, as Aron explains, there are numerous misconceptions about people who, as she describes, "just feel more deeply."

Below are 11 things you probably thought wrong about highly sensitive people.

1. They're weak.

As a society, we tend to rank people based on certain characteristics -- and HSPs tend to evade those traits that are perceived as "strong." "There are different kinds of weakness," Aron told The Huffington Post. "They're more sensitive to pain, so they're going to avoid a fight; that might make them look weak because they're not aggressive. They have more emotional reactivity, so they cry more easily."

But their ability to pick up on others' emotions and intuitive nature offers a different type of advantage, Aron explains. "Highly sensitive people see things in a way that other people don't see," she said. "It's a different kind of strength."

2. They're introverts.

High sensitivity is often used synonymously with introversion, but while they share similar characteristics (like wanting downtime and having relatively quiet personalities), Aron says the two are not the same. In fact, approximately 30 percent of HSPs are extroverts, according to her research.

3. They're easily offended.

Sensitive people cringe over criticism, and when they receive it, it's something they reflect on internally rather than take as a personal offense. Because they try to avoid scrutiny at all costs, HSPs tend to criticize themselves first or avoid the source of criticism altogether.

4. They're shy.

One of the largest misconceptions about the personality trait is that people perceive HSPs as shy or neurotic individuals, Aron says. This could partially be due to their aversion to criticism or their reserved nature -- but Aron stresses it's important to distinguish the differences. "Shy is a fear of social evaluation, and we are not born with that fear," she said. "A lot of people study shyness today and they don't realize what's under the hood, they just look at the behavior."

5. All highly sensitive people are women.

Sensitivity doesn't discriminate based on height, weight, gender, or job description. According to Aron, there are just as many men who possess the trait as there are women. "Being a sensitive man is difficult in our culture, but they are out there," she said. "There's no difference in how big and strong and masculine looking you are, if you're a man or a woman. It's not a matter of size."

6. They're prone to mental or physical illness.

Just like many other traits, it all comes down to variability in your genetics and environment. On average, a highly sensitive person is not at any more risk for mental or physical health issues, Aron says. In fact, if you're in a stabilized environment, the trait may even benefit you. "You're healthier than other people mentally and physically," she explained.

Aron also notes that the trait is not associated with the autism spectrum, like many people believe. Becoming easily overstimulated is a common thread -- especially in young children -- but she stresses that there are many other distinctions that parents should pay attention to and discuss with their doctor. "That's a difficult diagnosis to make in a very young child ... it's been misdiagnosed both ways, but they're different," she said.

7. Being highly sensitive negatively affects workplace success.

Because they're so intuitive, Aron says that sensitive individuals can actually use their trait to perform better. "It's not a handicap in relationships or at work," she said. "Sensitive people can use their observations to their advantage ... They're going to rise to the top. They know how to bring ideas up without being ridiculed or scorned."

8. They don't like big crowds.

While highly sensitive people do prefer to participate in activities (like exercise) solo, that doesn't mean they don't enjoy a large party or interacting in a big gathering. In fact, HSPs can thrive when there's social stimulation and some even find calm in large groups, Aron says.

9. They don't take risks.

It's a myth that highly sensitive individuals just want to stay at home or want everything calm and quiet all the time. Many HSPs seek high-sensation thrills like surfing and extensive traveling. Aron says they also choose careers where they can apply their traits while still finding stimulation and meaning, such as journalism or other service-based jobs.

10. You can easily identify a highly sensitive person.

In most cases, you probably won't be able to spot an HSP in a crowd, Aron explains. Save for a few eccentricities, like preferring alone time or a quiet restaurant over a noisy one, the personality trait doesn't often stand out. "They blend," she said. "They're creative, insightful and have a lot of empathy. People tend to like them."

11. The trait is abnormal.

Aron, who has been researching HSPs since the early '90s, says that nearly one in five people possess it. If you're interested in finding out if you're a highly sensitive person, you can take the self-assessment here: http://hsperson.com/test/highly-sensitive-test/.

A Highly Sensitive Entrepreneur?

As long as I can remember, I have felt different from everybody else. When my teacher asked me in high school what I wanted to be when I grew up, I always answered, "Happy, I just want to be happy when I grow up." I thought it was a great way to be all the time and wanted that to extend into my adult life too. However, I needed to decide what to "do" to be able to support myself or at least financially contribute to a household.

My particular road to discovering what career path to go on had a lot of different twist and turns. One of my favorite poems is from Robert Frost.

The Road Not Taken,
"Two roads diverged in a wood, and I—
I took the one less traveled by,
And that has made all the difference."

By the time I had my second child, I knew that I badly wanted to stay home and raise my beautiful daughter, Jennifer, and my newborn son, Joseph, myself. Taking them to a babysitter killed me every day. Yet, I also needed to help out with the added expenses that went along with a new baby. I opened a licensed day care center in our home and that's when I realized that being an entrepreneur was perfect for me and my family.

It was a perfect decision. I was able to make some money doing what I loved. It took me a quite a few years to realize why I loved being self-employed. I was actually into my next career, a hair stylist, when it hit me one day.

As a new stylist, I felt that I needed to work for a company and be on commission. It's a good way to get the money rolling in while you're building a clientele.
About six months into this "job," my energy was zapped all the time. I felt like I had no control and that

I was being forced to be around other people and social interactions plus environmental annoyances like chemical smells and loud noises.

All I wanted to do was the art and creativity of hairstyling. I realized I was never going to find the perfect job working for somebody else.
I was never going to be happy with a set schedule and set work. I stayed with this company just long enough to get some additional education, be financially stable, and then set out on my own as a highly successful entrepreneurial hairstylist.

Why HSP Are Designed For Self-Employment

The best career for a Highly Sensitive Person is one where they control every aspect of the environment.
The truth is, Highly Sensitive People are coded to be extremely successful within the world of self-employment.
According to Dr. Elaine N. Aron, one of the primary researchers of the high sensitivity personality trait and author of the book, *The Highly Sensitive Person*. She refers to this as the "advisor role" within society. She states, "For aggressive societies to survive, they always need that priest - judge - advisor class. Highly sensitive persons tend to fill that advisor role.
We are the writers, historians, philosophers, judges, artists, researchers, theologians, therapist, [coaches], teachers, parents, and plain conscientious citizens.

What we bring to any of these roles is a tendency to think about all the possible effects of an idea."
However, as Dr. Aron states, "to perform our role well, we have to feel very good about ourselves. We have

to ignore all the messages from the 'Warriors' that we are not as good as they are. The Warriors have their bold style, which has its value. But we, too, have our style and our own important contribution to make."

The key is, how do we do that? How do you use your unique highly sensitive abilities to support you in being purposeful, profitable, and empowered rather than scattered, poor, and undervalued?

Maybe you think being self-employed sounds impossible, or is only for 20-year old whiz kids or stay-at-home-moms or people doing some kind of shady "scam" business. But it's not true.

I know a lot of people who have created their own businesses and are doing very, very well.
These folks control everything, plus they have the excitement and fulfillment of being as creative as they want. They have the freedom to work when they want, where they want (including anywhere in the world).

Why I Do What I Do

In the beginning, they probably will work more hours

than the typical employee, but the difference is that they love what they do. There are lots of resources on the internet about how to create your own business.

An HSP will say, "I don't want to waste any more time or money on trying to figure it out on my own." But the real question HSPs ask me is, "How will I know which career or business is the right one for me?"

The answer to this question is exactly why I am coaching and mentoring people just like you. To help HSPs find the career, business, or job that best suits their strengths and unique abilities. It is also why I encourage HSPs to look at Network Marketing as a way to fulfill all their needs.

What Exactly Is Network Marketing?

Simply stated, Network Marketing is marketing a product or service by marketing through a network of people. Think *beyond* the people that you personally know. Think about the people that *they* know. Studies have shown that people will buy a product or service from a personal referral a lot faster and be more satisfied than through other types of advertising.

It is the best way, in my opinion, for an HSP to have a business because we are highly relational people and we appreciate the concept of compounding effect coupled with the incredible support and systems.

Network Marketing is another term that is used to describe Multi-Level Marketing or Direct Sales. There are thousands of these companies out there and unless you live under a rock, you've probably been invited to a networking meeting of some sort. Perhaps you've already personally experienced joining a company and been successful or disappointed. I myself can count on one hand the number of Direct Sales companies I've joined and quit. It was either the product/service was not a good fit for me, the timing was not right, or the company itself was shady.

This is what I have learned and truly believe. When a great product and great leadership come together, business miracles happen.

And this is why my husband and I are partners with some amazing companies.

Your Comfort Zone Is Your Broke Zone!

The biggest ongoing challenge that an HSP has in being self-employed is that our emotional skin is very thin.

- We don't like it when people tell us no.
- Trying to connect with a lot of new people is exhausting.
- Setting a goal is super scary.

We tend to make decisions based on how we feel about something. The problem with that is the decision is based on a past memory of a success or failure. In today's business world, changes happen so fast that we can't afford to rely on what used to work. We have to continually think outside the box for what will work with marketing and promotion, so that our voices will be heard.

This is exactly why HSPs are especially good at being Network Marketing Entrepreneurs. You get to call the shots and be in control of your financial destiny. Yet, there is a struggle that goes on inside us. Where is the balance of taking care of our needs and being a successful businessperson?

This is the very core of what I have worked on for over two years. You see, in my past, I have always been able to quickly rise to the financial top of my career choices. Yet when I look back at my career history, I see that after about ten years, I quit. Why would I leave something where I was good at what I did and made a lot of money doing it? Then the answer came to me. I was not fulfilled. I let myself become overwhelmed and exhausted because I ignored my highly sensitive nature.

Ask yourself this, "What is it that I could do that makes me fulfilled?"

For me, and I suspect most HSPs, the questions are

as complex as the answers. Since one of our traits is to be deep thinkers and feelers, we can use this to get the best possible answers.

"What is it about being fulfilled that is important to me?"

"Who do I have to become to get what I want and need?"

Can you see how these questions are going to reveal deeper thoughts and better answers? What has been revealed for me is that I wanted to be comfortable (who wouldn't) yet I also desired to be challenged (a human need).

As a result, my comfort zone became my broke zone.

Until My BIG WHY became larger than my fear.

What Is A Big Why? It is the reason that drives you to jump out of bed in the morning with excitement. It is why you keep doing what you do regardless of what other people think or tell you.

It is a calling so profound and so deep that nothing will stop you from pursuing it.

This book was written as part of my big why. It has been extremely uncomfortable to write about my personal life struggles knowing that the whole world was now going to see more of me. To step through the fear and find on the other side that I am meant to help other people heal and have extraordinary lives.

My Big Why is to be a History Changer. To teach, mentor, guide and coach other Highly Sensitive People that are struggling so that they can thrive in the chaotic world.

By sharing my stories my hope is that you will learn more about yourself and what you want for your life.

***

"Choose a job you love, and you will never have to work a day in your life." **–Confucius**

I keep both of these quotes on my heart and go to them whenever I feel my old fears creep in.

"Life Begins At The Edge Of Your Comfort Zone." **–Tony Robbins**

***

Overwhelm Hurts

Later in this book, you will read about my health and healing challenge and what I learned about HSP's sensitivities to our environment and decisions we make that get us into overwhelm.

It hurts physically and emotionally. It can give us chronic health conditions and it's the cause of us not living up to our beautiful potential.

It takes away the one thing that HSPs truly desire — to be fulfilled. It keeps us away from those we enjoy helping and our true nature of being a servant leader.

Journal
What do you feel is the ideal career for you?

Chapter Two

Define Your Abilities

Earlier in Chapter One, I shared with you *11 Things Everyone Gets Wrong About Highly Sensitive People.* In this chapter, I am going to show you how to define your abilities so that you will learn how to use them in your world.

Take special note of what Dr. Jeffrey E. Young, an American psychologist best known for having developed the schema therapy, has to say about the importance of focusing on what your needs are first. Something especially hard for us to do. This I know and now finally understand deeply — I cannot be the person that God created, the shining light of faith, love, hope, and kindness for others, if I give up all of me in the shadow of serving.

Psychologist Elaine Aron writes in her book, *The Highly Sensitive Person,* that about 15 to 20 percent of the population is characterized as highly sensitive (HS). She adds that about 30 percent of people are moderately sensitive, while 50 percent of people think of themselves as being sensitive while they are "not at all sensitive."

What being highly sensitive is NOT:

- Emotionally immature
- Self-centered
- Unpredictable and unstable emotions
- Over-dependent
- Demanding and attention-thirsty

Characteristics of highly sensitive people:

- Have great imagination
- Have great intellectual abilities
- Are creative
- Have a curious mind
- Are hard workers
- Are good problem solvers
- Are extremely conscious and compassionate
- Are intuitive, caring, and spiritual
- Have a strong sense of aesthetic awareness
- Respect nature, art, and music greatly
- Have profound and intense sensations
- Can access important information from the unconscious mind
- Have a depth of understanding and feelings
- Are objective and can see the bigger picture

If Highly Sensitive People don't learn to handle their high sensitivity, they may suffer greatly. Some of these are a loss of balance when it comes to a self-sacrifice schema (a schema is an organized pattern of thought and behavior), which always leads to emotional deprivation. For instance, Dr. Jeffrey E. Young links high sensitivity, or as he calls it, the "highly empathic temperament," with the Self-Sacrifice Schema, which in turn is almost always related to the Emotional Deprivation Schema. In his opinion, these individuals need to learn to focus on themselves instead of or before focusing on others, and they need to learn to get their own needs met first, needs they typically are not aware of. After that self-understanding, they will have a clear picture of what they want to do to make a difference with their life.

Journal
Have you had an "Aha" moment?

5 Ways That Can Help HS People Manage Their Abilities

Emotionally, highly sensitive individuals are easily overstimulated up to a point where they may experience great joy or great pain. They can have a combination of an introvert and an extrovert personality traits due to the fact that they need to be by themselves to become centered, and they also love connecting to other people and their environment. As reported before, many of these people learn to mask this gift of sensitivity, intuition, and creativity because they do not know how to deal with the overstimulation.

Physically, highly sensitive people need time and space to be by themselves to process the amount of input they absorb. They may have low tolerance to noise and anything too strong when it comes to sensations. They also seem to have more body awareness and can feel when their body is not comfortable in an environment. Therefore, nutritionally, they have to stick to simple foods that are full of nutrients and have a healthy balance. They also have to connect to nature and do regular exercise, relaxation, meditation, and any other activities that go with their nature to calm themselves down and recharge after the over stimulation.

Socially, sometimes HS people may feel like misfits and have to learn ways to tolerate imperfections they see in the depth of others. They need to learn to connect while having clear boundaries as to when to say no and how far to go with something and someone. In addition, HS people need to become assertive and have regular "me" times. When it comes to their social personality, these individuals are usually shy, but their shyness is not because they are weak but rather is based on a need to survive. Since their nature is oversensitive, biologically they are designed to be shy as a self-protection mode. However, if the shyness is too much and is affecting their need to be social and to connect, then they can modify it through behavioral and cognitive modification.

Additionally, they have to learn to give and receive love and they have to realize that the process has to have a balance point. They have to understand that self-sacrifice that leads to emotional deprivation is not healthy. They have to allow themselves to be vulnerable, face problems rather than running away from them, relate positively to life, and learn from their experiences. Some of these individuals avoid some areas of their life and some of the challenges because of their oversensitivity not realizing that in some of these challenges lies great opportunity.

And last but not least, these individuals have to find a meaning in their life. All humanity desires this, but

for highly sensitive people, this is a *need*.
It is their innermost desire to help others be happy, and they can use their abilities to bring their creative side out and make this world a better place for all, even if a small step.

Overall, many of our writers, creators, inventors, imaginaries, discoverers, and people who have contributed greatly to this world may fall in the category of highly sensitive. We need more of these people and we need to encourage them to unleash their potential. For those people who want to become more sensitive, they have to learn ways to overcome society's encouragement to be overly analytical, materialistic, and competitive, and to encourage themselves and others to cherish this trait and make the best of it.

Journal
What helps you manage your abilities?

"Isn't it Just Feminine Energy?"

The other day I was eating lunch with some friends at an event.

Most of my friends are open to new progressive ideas and are educated in human psychology. Like me, they are always curious about life experiences and are what we call *lifelong learners*.

As we were joyfully sharing what we were up to lately, I opened up with the concept of writing this book to address the challenges highly sensitive people face in today's world.

Being curious, they wanted to know more about what was a Highly Sensitive Person. I suspect that they wanted to know if they were Highly Sensitive. In the middle of my explanation of the traits and abilities that an HSP has, I was suddenly stopped by one of my friends and asked, "Isn't that just feminine energy?"

This is not the first time I have been asked that. In fact, it is a frequently asked question.

It seems whenever I am talking to someone that is not Highly Sensitive, they just don't get it.
If the term feminine energy is new to you, then I have

some good news for you. I'm going to share with you, to the best of my ability, what it is and how it differs from being an HSP.

In the first chapter you read what the definition of a HSP is. And by now, perhaps, you have even gone to Elaine Aron's website and taken the self-assessment. If you need a refresher, I invite you to check out chapter one again.

Feminine Energy

Everyone has both a masculine and a feminine side. For the purpose of this chapter, I am leaving out the masculine explanation because I will only be comparing feminine energy and a Highly Sensitive Person at this time.

Being an HSP is not exclusive to women. There are just as many men that are born with the traits as there are women. But society dictates that men are not supposed to possess the traits and women are. Both will suffer and be confused by this stereotyping.

As in most things, there are varying degrees of feminine energy depending on the individual person, the culture they are living in, how they were raised as a child, and their hormones.

The feminine side is based on a deep level of the

value that you place on others. If you have a strong feminine side and place a high value on others, you are often giving and unselfish.

You usually know what is good for people, and you tend to operate in ways that help others get what they want out of life. People feel comfortable around you because you give of who you are without pushing yourself on others.

Conversely, if you have a weak feminine side, you place a low value on others and you are not a giving person. You are isolated because you don't want to share yourself or share anything you have. Also, you don't take responsibility for actions and place blame on others for your problems.

A strong feminine energy often behaves in ways that are considered feminine in nature. You will do things that are giving and unselfish. This includes recognizing people's basic human rights and allowing them to live their life without interfering with those rights. Allowing people their basic rights includes letting them control their own life, letting them choose what they want to believe without being manipulated by you.

The feminine side also includes having an enthusiasm and zest for life, and recognizing what things are worth getting enthusiastic about.

It also includes being kind, compassionate, patient, and responsive to the needs of others, and it includes the ability to limit the amount of energy you put into helping people, to keep from hurting yourself or draining your own energy.

There is a gathering aspect to feminine energy, going back to the cavemen days where the hunters (men) went out with their physical strength, spears, knives, and arrows to hunt for food and protect the family.

The women, and weak men and children, would stay close to the cave and gather food from the ground, bushes, and trees. They had to remember the details of where to find non-poisonous berries and clean water. They would stay close together to protect each other from a pouncing tiger or lion.

These are the basic needs for survival even to this day. Feminine energy today is still about gathering and staying together for survival and protection. It's just looks a little bit different. In today's world, we see survival as being accepted into the group. We will gather together for lunch and give kind words and support even if we don't mean it.

An all important thing that happy and healthy feminine energy gathers and shares are details — details about a person, a dress, a pair of shoes, who was at the party or a trip — and when the time is right, she will share them until your ears fall off.

Now let's go back and do some comparing to the HSP and connect the dots.

What being highly sensitive is NOT:

- Emotionally immature
- Self-centered
- Unpredictable and unstable emotions
- Over-dependent
- Demanding and attention-thirsty

Characteristics of highly sensitive people:

- Have great imagination
- Have great intellectual abilities
- Are creative
- Have a curious mind
- Are hard workers
- Are good problem solvers
- Are extremely conscious and compassionate
- Are intuitive, caring and spiritual
- Have a strong sense of aesthetic awareness
- Respect nature, art, and music greatly
- Have profound and intense sensations
- Can access important information from the unconscious mind
- Have a depth of understanding and feelings
- Are objective and can see the bigger picture

A Highly Sensitive Person has similar traits to feminine energy when it comes to being conscious, caring, and compassionate. There is also a correlation to having a strong sense of aesthetic awareness (shoes and outfit matching), and the ability to access important information from the unconscious mind (intuition). Other than that, there is not much else in common. Go ahead and take a few moments to jot down your feelings about the feminine energy you have versus what your HSP qualities are.

Journal

The Shadow Side To High Sensitivity

When I first heard about the shadow side of being an HSP, I was surprised and intrigued. For a minute, I rejected the whole concept and even said to myself, "That would not even apply to me. I know myself all too well."
But my curiosity and desire to learn more got me to take a look at the "shadows."

What is a shadow? A very simple way to explain what an actual shadow is, is this: It is our darkness that is hidden and unseen by us when we are facing a light. We can only see it when we turn around, away from the light, and there it is.

By shadow, I do not refer to the problems we are all familiar with, but rather those that might be stuffed out of sight — as if seeing them would be too painful. It won't be. You'll see.

We Can Sure Be Critical
So what might these shadow aspects be? Well, first, we can see into anything with such skill that we can't help noticing the flaws. Since we also have a deep need to be kind, we often keep our critiques to ourselves, but in certain situations we let loose. Some might do this with their spouse or their children. I do it when I'm tired or overwhelmed.

Being A Sensitive Doormat

Another word for this would be pushover. Please notice this may not be an issue for you at all. These are just possibilities, knowing how we are. This would be described as giving in too easily, or being defeated. Being submissive, subservient, weak. Not physically, but socially.

We may call our "giving in" just being nice or showing our empathy, or we may say we don't care or it isn't worth the hassle to get our way, but this feeling of being inferior keeps us from speaking our mind or being treated fairly.

We might overextend our time with people, giving into the other person's desires even though we wanted to leave an hour ago. We will commit to helping someone out then feel bad when we begin to see that they might be taking advantage of our kindness. It just happened to me the other day. I had left a question on a voicemail for someone that did not get back to me. When I saw her a few days later, she explained that she had gotten the message but only had time to return the calls of the cranky people, that I was so nice she felt I would understand.

Yes, I am nice. Because I will always believe that you will get more with honey than vinegar, but when I need to be firm with someone, I will not hesitate to tell someone in kindness, "Please do not mistake my kindness for weakness."

One of the most valuable lessons that I learned while I was studying grief counseling was that people will always need a L.E.G. (Little Extra Grace).

Fear Of Vulnerability

I get a great deal of pleasure taking care of people. It also happens to be a positive quality of an HSP. Doing something for someone actually increases our endorphins and serotonin levels, those feel good hormones.

The shadow of this is that I do not want to show that I am weak or vulnerable because it would mean that people could not depend on my strength. Yet, when I give so much that my body does a crash and burn, then I resent giving so much. It is something I work on every day.

This shadow can result from the treatment we receive for being highly sensitive and might be the way we compensate for feeling not respected, unappreciated, and even ashamed.

We might seem indifferent, which can look like or become arrogance and significance driven.

A coldness about us will tell others that we don't care, yet that is just a cover to protect us.

Striving to always be on top, the best, can look like or become ruthlessness, one-sidedness — again, a loss of feeling for others. Trying to prove our worth, we may just work ourselves into the ground, caring nothing for our own body's feelings.

How can an HSP do any of that? Easy. Shame and rejection are horrible, horrible feelings. The unconscious mind will take control to protect us from the worst.

So, quite involuntarily, we may make it our highest priority to avoid this agony.

I find, even in myself, that people will always do more to avoid pain than to gain pleasure.

Indecisiveness

I have a saying that I use whenever I feel pressure to make a decision. "Do it once, do it right." I always thought it was because I didn't want to waste precious time, energy, and resources redoing it. I believe that the best outcomes come from having all the information that I need to make the best decision.

Elaine Aron says it like this: "One reason HSPs

evolved to be so reflective is that our strategy allows us to survive better when our environment is in a dangerous phase — for example, if there are more predators around this year (or we're in a "bear market"), or there's not much food until the rains come so, to avoid eating just anything and being sickened, you have to choose carefully (or pay attention to the nutritional contents on the packages). But eventually we have to act. Do something. Eat. We have to take a risk."

Irritability

My cup runneth over. My tanks are empty. The basket is full. Stick me with a fork, I'm done.
All things I've said to people, and myself, when I can't take it one more second.

How about the times when we just want to crawl into a corner or under the blankets and say, "Go away"?

There is a tipping point to pay attention to and it is always a moving target. If you happen to wake up tired because you didn't sleep well. Ate something that didn't agree with you. Committed to doing too much.

And all the people in your life see you as strong keep asking you for more.

There comes a time when sometimes we just lose it when we don't want anything from anyone except maybe to be left alone.

An ugly shadow is that we try to control ourselves for just a little longer, because we are so sensitive to other people's needs but ignore our own. We may even explode on someone. Do we secretly enjoy the explosions? Do we take responsibility for what we did or didn't do to let our over-arousal happen?

Being Too Trusting, Then Too Shocked

On the subject of expecting others to be like us, I have found many HSPs just quietly do their jobs, expecting others to notice and appreciate them. Expecting the world to be just. Sometimes it works well. But more often, no acknowledgment happens and the person who "tooted his own horn" without doing half as much gets the praise and the raise. Then the HSP is shocked, bitter, becomes cynical, maybe passive aggressive, coming late to work and so forth. The shadow of our conscientiousness and modesty is our secret belief that it should be rewarded.

We have to remember that non-HSPs do not notice subtleties! They do not respond to hints! And they can mistake conscientiousness for all sorts of things.

So, use your deeper processing to notice if you are not being noticed, and see that you are.

Being Eccentric And Fussy

Finally, for all of our ability to sense what's going on around us, we can get out of touch with reality if we spend too much time alone, protecting ourselves from over-stimulation. We have to remain part of society if we are going to do it any good, so find ways that are comfortable for you to stay in touch with the news, with the latest fashions in this and that, with the interests of other generations, other ethnicities. It will mean that your intuition in any given situation will be more accurate. You can't process what you haven't taken in, in some way.

That was not so bad, was it? And becoming more aware of even one aspect of one's shadow makes us a broader person, as well as one less judgmental of others.

Here's the good and the bad of shadows. They are predictable and will always be there where you can expect them. Like a best friend that you don't really like, but because you know each other so well, you will never really be rid of them.

Get to know your shadows and understand that they are part of the human being that you are. Be the HSP that you are and be kind to yourself and others.

Consider the Fruits of the Spirit

But the fruit of the Spirit is Love, Joy, Peace, Patience, Kindness, Goodness, Faithfulness, Gentleness, and Self-Control... Galatians 5:22-23

Journal
Can you think of ways to appreciate your shadows?

The Highly Sensitive Person In A Relationship

In my marriage, I am often frustrated when my husband will say something that causes me stress. I am constantly weighing whether he is being masculine, which I honor and even celebrate, or is he being an insensitive jerk doing bad behavior. ;)

He has a habit of judging other people's behavior to me. He feels this is a safe way to complain. He can get his frustrations with other people off his chest in a safe place where they can't hear him. This is a masculine trait with a non-confrontational behavior. What he doesn't understand is that because of my HSP trait, I will take it on as if he is judging me and/or I will unconsciously feel in the pit of my stomach and deep in my heart the pain the other person would feel from such unheard criticism.

I do enough judging on myself, listening to the ideal women in my head, that when he does this it adds jet fuel to the fire and I feel attacked. He is not aware he is doing it and does not intentionally want to hurt me. He is just not using a filter of sensitivity before he says something. I bite my tongue most of the time so that he can be his true, authentic self. But it is eventually exhaustive and overwhelming for me so I will ask him to stop. The poor man probably feels at times that he can't say anything around me.

I practice and pray every day for patience for myself and for him. I love this passage from the Bible; "I pray that your heart will be flooded with light so that you can see something of the future that God has called you to share." Ephesians 1:18

Turns out, there's nothing really wrong with me and there's nothing wrong with him — I am just a highly sensitive person.

He loves all of me — I just see that he gets confused with some of my parts of being a sensitive person. I have finally come to the realization that Michael will never see the depth of something like I do. The way I deeply ponder something, a statement, the color of a plant, the beauty of a stone, even a decision on where we might have dinner. And it's not because he doesn't care — it's because he can't and he never will see as deeply.

My releasing this expectation of him has had a profound effect on our relationship. For the last couple of years, I found myself being critical of him and then feeling deeply confused for it. I was always correcting him on what he did not see or hear. For instance, not too long ago he made a negative comment about a driver of a car that apparently stopped in the middle of the street for no reason, causing him to abruptly stomp on the brakes. What I saw was that the driver stopped to avoid hitting a bicyclist.

I have had numerous conversations and requests for Michael about how, as an HSP, when I overhear any judgements placed on other people, I will take them on myself and even go as far as unconsciously believing that I will be the next one in line to be attacked. I will admit that this trait may not be true for other HSPs, and it is based on my personal experience of being a victim of abuse and from learning that this is also common in a vast majority of my coaching clients.

Journal

8 Surprising Facts About Highly Sensitive Spouses

I want to share with you an excerpt from a recent article I found by author Chaunie Brusie, an HSP herself.

"I recently had the opportunity to chat with Dr. Aron, a self-professed highly sensitive person and author of The Highly Sensitive Person In Love, and her social psychologist husband, Arthur, who identifies as a non-highly sensitive person, about the topic as they spent a quiet afternoon at home working on holiday cards. According to them, about 20% of the population can be classified as "highly sensitive," a genetic trait that affects how information is processed in the brain — and can also highly affect relationships. Here are 8 important things I took away from the conversation:

1. **Highly sensitive spouses may not know that they are highly sensitive.**

One of the biggest sources of frustration for highly sensitive people, notes Dr. Aron, is that they are often times not even aware that they are highly sensitive — which can cause issues to arise, particularly in marriage. But there are clues that spouses can look for to help discern if his or her partner is highly sensitive, using the acronym DOES — Depth of Processing, Over-stimulated, Empathy and Emotional

Responsiveness, and Subtle Stimuli.

"A highly sensitive person thinks deeply ... they think about the meaning of life more, they are the ones in the family who make sure they get their health check-ups," Dr. Aron rattles off. "If you have children, they are the ones who run out of the room first. With husbands — they are often in their offices; for mothers, they look like they are going crazy."

2. Highly sensitive spouses need alone time.

Highly sensitive people, like introverts (although the two are not interchangeable), often have a deep need for alone time, to allow their brain ample time to process, a situation that can cause frustration among married partners. When a highly sensitive spouse feels the need for downtime, Dr. Aron suggests making ones needs known — and being very clear about it. "You can just say, 'I'm taking some down time, this is how long I will be gone,' " she says.

And Arthur chimes in with the importance of making it clear that you are not wanting time away from your spouse — but just time away from, well, everyone. The couple also advises exploring ways to get down time together through quiet activities, such as hiking or sitting together reading.

3. Men are just as likely to be highly sensitive as women.

"As many men as women are born sensitive, but the stereotype is that women are sensitive, 'real' men are not," Dr. Aron explains on her website. Arthur also points out that cultural norms influence how we view sensitive males, referencing a study that showed that in Canada, highly sensitive boys were ranked as the least popular, while in China, the most sensitive young males were also the most popular.

4. Highly sensitive people view sex differently.

"HSPs are more likely to find sex to be mysterious and powerful, to be turned on by subtle rather than explicit sexual cues, to be easily distracted or physically hurt during sex, and to find it difficult to go right back to normal life afterwards," says Dr. Aron on her site. Keeping an open communication going in — and out — of the bedroom can help explore some of those different needs.

5. Bedtime might be a particular crisis.

In her book, Dr. Aron uses an anecdote of bedtime to illustrate the differences between an HS and non-HS spouse — she climbs into bed only to find her brain is too overly-stimulated to sleep, while her husband is quietly snoring within minutes. I found myself nodding along vigorously because that is my life.

For example, my husband loves unwinding with TV before bed, but I find it way too stimulating.

This always places me in the dilemma of whether to spend time with my husband before bed or take my own down time away from screens?

I usually go back and forth, but more often than not, I just can't shut down my own brain without a nice, dark room and no screens in my presence.

6. Highly sensitive people make good decisions.

If you have a highly sensitive spouse, you may want to defer to them for decision-making, because Dr. Aron explains that although highly-sensitive people can take longer to make decisions, "they're usually good ones." She may, for instance, recall some unpleasant details about a restaurant they are considering eating at, or avoid a certain hiking trail based on past experiences, saving both parties the bane of bad bread or a less-than-dazzling view.

7. Fighting warrants special consideration for highly sensitive people.

It's not a stretch to imagine that if one or both partners are highly sensitive in a marriage, fights *could have the potential for disaster, but the Aron's have a few tips for making it through intact.*

"For sensitive people, when you get to the point where you're really over aroused, stop and take a 20-minute break," Dr. Aron advises. Or better yet, try not to get to that point.
She also suggests staying on the topic of what you are discussing. "Don't start bringing up the other things you're mad at your partner for," she says. "If you're discussing how your children should be educated, you don't want to bring up the subject of how their mother didn't do things right." If you start throwing in what Dr. Aron dubs, "the kitchen sink," then everything escalates.

Being highly sensitive also might mean being more vulnerable to slights by your partner — the person who knows you best in the world.

"The whole goal for humans is not to be shamed — your partner knows you so well that it's easy for them to bring up the things that are shameful," she notes.

8. Recognizing that you're highly sensitive won't magically fix your marriage.

Although it may feel like a bit of an eye-opener, a spouse recognizing that he or she is highly sensitive won't magically transform a relationship overnight. "Couples need to get it that it's genetics, you can't change this about your partner — but you can change how you manage it," Dr. Aron says. "If you don't get that, you become a hard person to live with."

So what's a newly informed Highly Sensitive Spouse supposed to do with all of this enlightenment? "Don't go running to your spouse with the good news," cautions Dr. Aron. "Don't expect your partner to be delighted with this news," she notes.

And of course, I dutifully recorded her advice — then went running to my husband with the news that I thought I was highly sensitive.

He looked at me skeptically.

"Highly sensitive, huh?" he scoffed. "I'd say more like highly egocentric."

I think he was just kidding.

And if he wasn't, don't tell me — I'm not sure I'll take the news well."

Journal
How would you communicate your HSP?

HSP And *6 Human Needs*

Life Will Never Be The Same Again

It was early March of 2002, a little bit after midnight near the Queen Mary in Long Beach, California. I was walking barefoot in the worst rain storm Southern California has ever had, and I was freaking out. I was about to walk over hot coals for the first time in my life and I was freaking out because I was getting soaking wet.

As you can imagine, this particular night changed my life forever.

Back up a few months to November, 2001. At that time, I had been working as a hairstylist for about six years. I loved every aspect of my career. Helping people look and feel their best. Creating works of art with hair and the constant education helped propel me to become one of the top Master stylists in the area. It was not unusual for me to pick up a new client every week or so. And that is how I met a client that would change my life forever. Fast forward to March, I was working on the hair of this new client when out of the blue she asked me if I wanted to attend a Tony Robbins four day *Unleash The Power Within* event. It was going to be in about a week and about 30 minutes from where I lived.

If you haven't heard of Tony Robbins, you can find out more at *TonyRobbins.com*.

Well, I hesitated and kinda said, "Ok?" when she stopped me and said, "Honey, if you say yes, then you have to go and I will get you a ticket."

Now, I had followed Tony Robbins and read his book and even had an old cassette tape that I enjoyed. I never thought I would end up at an event. And now I was standing there in the pouring rain looking down on really hot coals that I was about to walk on.

This turned out to be a major turning point in my life. And I thank God every day for all the events that had to happen for that client and me to come together.
Since that first event, and every year after that, I have enjoyed attending at least three or more of Tony's events as a crew member or a Senior Leader, helping support the transformation of thousands of people. I have also taken the steps toward joining Tony Robbins' coaching team as a certified Strategic Interventionist. I can truly say life has never been the same.

Because of what I have learned about human psychology and how to get people out of their pain fast, I have left the field of hair styling and am now a full time Life Success Coach and Strategic Interventionist.

How does a Highly Sensitive Person navigate all of this? That is exactly why I wrote this book. To help you understand that you too can have a life of meaning and fulfillment.

Tony Robbins has taken human psychology into his teachings and uses the six human needs to help understand how we make decisions in our lives.
I have hundreds of stories about how understanding these *6 HN's* have saved marriages, a relationship with a teenage child, a relationship between a coworker and a boss. I believe they change the course of history in people's lives.

All human beings share the same six basic human needs. These needs underlie all the choices we make in our lives.

CERTAINTY

The first need is for *Certainty*. We want to feel safe, avoid pain and feel comfortable in our environment and our relationships. Every individual needs to have some sense of certainty and security – a roof over one's head, knowing where the next meal will come from, knowing how to obtain care when one is sick, knowing that a neighbor won't attack us. These are just a few examples of what constitutes a basic sense of certainty.

Everyone needs certainty but the degree to which certainty is needed or desired varies from person to person. Some people feel secure living in one room and collecting an unemployment check. Others can feel certainty only if they make a million dollars each year. Even though some certainty is necessary to all of us, what constitutes certainty varies from individual to individual. Code words for *Certainty* are comfort, security, safety, stability, feeling grounded, predictability, and protection.

An HSP's need for certainty is especially high. Controlling their environment and other people can take on an obsessive quality if not kept in check with reality. There are extremes from one end of the spectrum to the other where one person may need to know every little detail about an upcoming trip to relieve their emotional stress and another HSP can relax with a limited amount of information knowing that whatever happens will be absolutely perfect. I see quite a few HSPs never having a long term, successful relationship with someone because there is no certainty in it. They will stay single the rest of their lives rather than take the risk of having an intimate relationship in their lives.

UNCERTAINTY/VARIETY

The second need is for *Uncertainty* – for variety and challenges that exercise our emotional and physical range. Everyone needs some variety in life. Our bodies, our minds, our emotional well-being all require uncertainty, exercise, suspense, and surprise.

Just as a sense of security is reassuring, so the excitement that comes from variety is necessary to feel alive. For some, variety may be satisfied by watching the news on television; others may seek extreme high-risk activities such as extreme sports. Code words for *Uncertainty/Variety* are: fear, thrills, instability, change, entertainment, suspense, exertion, surprise, conflict, and crisis.

To an HSP, having too much uncertainty and variety is overwhelming for them. It can be a major form of stress in their lives. Yet I know plenty of HSPs that have high energy jobs, careers, hobbies, and friends, and they do just fine. According to research, there is a subset of HSP. About 30% of all HSPs are to some degree known a High Sensation Seekers, or HSS.

I happen to score high as an HSS. I can get bored easily and want lots of variety. My challenge is to find a sweet spot where I don't bite off more than I can chew. In other words, I must not overcommit to doing something and then not be able to follow through because I got too overstimulated and exhausted.

SIGNIFICANCE

The third need is for *Significance*. Every person needs to feel important, needed, wanted. Significance comes from comparing ourselves to others – in our quest for significance, we are always involved in questions of superiority and inferiority. We can feel significant because we have achieved something, built something, succeeded at something, or we can seek significance by tearing down something or somebody.

In its positive aspect, significance leads us to raise our standards. But if we are overly focused on significance, we will have trouble truly connecting with others – comparisons focus on differences rather than commonalities. For some, significance comes from providing for the family; for others, from doing meaningful work. Some need to make a major contribution to the community, and some require considerable wealth. Some people achieve a sense of significance by failure, by being the worst at something, or by having low self-esteem. Whatever the measure of significance, a sense of being important is necessary to all human beings. Code words for *Significance* are: pride, importance, standards, achievement, performance, perfection, evaluation, discipline, competition, respect, and rejection.

In my experience, I have not seen very many HSPs that have a high need for significance. Just by our very nature, we tend to avoid standing out in a crowd asking to be seen more than other people. If you did run into someone that was seeking the center of attention, it is most likely because they fall into the category of a High Sensation Seeker (HSS), as I mentioned in Chapter One.

Some HSPs will take on the identity of "being" highly sensitive and use it as an excuse or reason to not do something. You will hear them say something like "I'm an HSP, I can't do that" or "can't go there" or "can't eat that." I am not suggesting that an HSP should do something that is uncomfortable or could trigger a crisis. I just encourage people to take the stance of "I don't **want** to do that." It's more powerful and honors your decisions to take care of yourself. For an HSP, significance is high when we compare ourselves to others. When I begin working with clients, the first thing I notice is how my client wants to know how to fit in with the rest of the world. They are struggling so much at work, in their business, and even at home. It seems to them that there is a constant battle trying to make sense with the chaos and crisis of their world. No wonder they are exhausted to the point of nonfunctioning.

LOVE/CONNECTION

The fourth need is for the experience of *Love and*

Connection. Everyone needs connection with other human beings and everyone strives for and hopes for love. An infant needs to be loved and cared for during a long period of time if it is to develop normally. Infants who are not held and touched will die.

This need for love continues throughout our lives. It is epitomized by the concept of romantic love, the one person who will devote their life to us and make us feel complete.

In some cultures, romantic love doesn't exist; it's replaced by the love of relatives, friends, and tribe.

Some people rarely experience love, but they have many ways of feeling connection with others – in the community or in the workplace. The need to be loved is characteristic of all human beings. Code words for *Love/Connection* are: togetherness, passion, unity, warmth, tenderness, and desire.

HSPs usually rate high for *Love and Connection,* yet what can happen is that they can fall victim to people taking advantage of their sensitivity to taking care of others. And the high need to be loved and to be enough for others will place them in the position of being a pleaser. This in turn can cause them to be doormats and controlled by others.

A healthy *Love/Connection* means that both parties are contributing to the relationship 100%, a partnership where your needs are my needs and my needs are your needs.

GROWTH

The fifth need is for *Growth*. When we stop growing, we die. We need to constantly develop emotionally, intellectually, and spiritually. We grow and change physically as we develop from infancy to adulthood and old age. We grow and change emotionally with every experience, and we grow intellectually as we respond to events and to the world around us.
Anything that you want to remain in your life – your money, your health, your relationship, your happiness, your love – must be cultivated, developed, expanded.
Otherwise, it will degenerate. Some people satisfy the need to grow by working out physically or by reading a book. Others need to study and learn constantly in order to feel that they are truly growing. Code words for *Growth* are: developing, learning, self-improvement, studying, and understanding.

In my research and experience, I see a lot of HSPs fall into *Growth* as a high need, especially if they are an introvert. There is a special quality about wanting to learn more and experience life deeply from the safety of a book or a computer. We have an inane curiosity to experience the imagination and fascination deeply that we can only get from a story.

We are lifelong learners and when we learn something, we want to share this with others. That is why you will find a lot of teachers that are HSP.

CONTRIBUTION

The sixth need is for *Contribution* – to go beyond our own needs and to give to others. A life is incomplete without the sense that one is making a contribution to others or to a cause. It is in the nature of human beings to want to give back, to leave a mark on the world. Giving to others may mean giving time to community service, making a charitable donation, planting trees, or giving to one's children.

Not only can everyone contribute in some way, but contribution is essential to a sense of fulfillment and to happiness.

Code words for *Contribution* are: giving, sharing, helping, supporting, guiding, teaching, and making a difference.

As I mention above about Growth, teaching is an inherent need for a HSP. Many of us are our happiest when we can contribute with our gifts and abilities. Many of us become educators, coaches, trainers, guides, mentors, or volunteers at our favorite charity or church. We feel deeply about a cause.

What needs to be addressed here is that when an HSP is giving their all to a person, family, or cause, then there will be nothing left of them. They will become completely exhausted and yet enjoy every moment. Without a balance and the skill to say NO to others, their high need to help others will finally take a toll on their health. I know about this one personally.

The Next Step

The first thing I do when I begin working with a new client is have them take the 84 question assessment so that we both know where they are at in regard to their own *6 Human Needs*. This helps me coach them through any conflicts they are having with themselves and the relationships they have with others. If you want more information, please contact me at www.WonderfulLifeLearning.com and I will be honored to work with you or someone that you feel needs help.

So now it's your turn to journal about what the *6 Human Needs* mean in your life.

Journal
Which ones do you feel are your top two needs that drive your daily decisions?

Chapter Three

How To Exist In The Chaotic World

I've often wondered if I am going crazy.

Even though I loved my profession as a hairstylist, for over 15 years, I hated working in a salon. For what was a normal salon environment turned into torture for me.

The strong odors of perms, nails, and color chemicals hit me whenever I first walked into work. The physical exhaustion that would overwhelm me after 10 hours on my feet, the lack of privacy and the onslaught of the blow dryers, the constant chatter and overhead music cranked up all around me. Not to mention the artificial, fluorescent light that buzzed overhead all day.
Even after I eventually found a salon where I could work near a window for natural light, it still was not enough and I ultimately retired from the business after over 15 years.

The physical pain that I was constantly experiencing from this onslaught was making me resent the very clients that I loved to take care of.

Through my coaching practice, I came to realize a pattern developing where my clients were experiencing the same frustrations and pain that I was. Knowing that like attracts like, I began to pay attention to what was showing up in my clients.

I noticed that some of my clients were super sensitive to some things, like the sadness of their children, where others were not. But then some were sensitive to their physical surroundings to the point of obsession.

This led me to study what it means to be a highly sensitive person.

I have read and studied virtually everything I could get my hands on. Much of it on the internet, some of it from suggestions from friends, but most of it has come from Dr. Elaine Aron and her studies that began in the early '90s.

Psychologist Elaine Aron has pioneered the study of a category of human personality that is generating considerable buzz both in the media and in the scientific community: the highly sensitive person (HSP).
People in this group look the same as everyone else, but they don't respond to the world the same. The way they think, work, feel, and even love is
distinctive. Tendencies like acute awareness of

emotions, heightened response to loud noises and other stimuli, and the deep processing of information are all things that set HSPs apart.

Now that I am coaching full time, I am much happier. I can control my environment, most of the time. I have a small and lovely home office where I do much of my coaching in. There is soft flowing curtains on the window that allow just enough afternoon light in. I don't have a lot of distractions (what I call bright shiny objects), with the exception of a small ceramic bowl that I made in high school, full of my favorite polished stones and seashells that I found on the beach. I have a small, brand new, low maintenance plant by the window.

It is a little too cluttered right now yet it doesn't seem to bother me. It's full of stuff I love.

When I go out to my weekly marketing meetings is when I can have challenges. Sometimes I won't even go If I don't like the venue.

An example: One of the networking meetings I joined and was a member of for over a year changed their meeting place.
When I arrived, it was an open space, more industrial, with high ceilings in the area where a kitchen table was. We all brought food and congregated around that kitchen table for attempted conversation. I say "attempted" because all the sound

traveled up and bounced off the metal ceiling back down onto us. The more women that arrived, the worse it got until I had to leave the area.

I have realized that If I am distracted and drained by my environment I cannot put my best foot forward for networking.

I make no apologies for leaving a gathering early if I am uncomfortable. When I first arrive at an event, I check out the space before I settle in, noticing the energy of the people and the room. I will always try to sit near a window facing the room. I don't like people coming up behind me; it can be startling when I suddenly feel someone's energy before I see them. A window will allow me to tap into the nature outside for grounding.

This is not being a snob or picky. I call this being discerning about what I need to notice so that I will be able to use my HSP abilities. It's about me finally taking care of what I need to be able to serve others. It is preventing chaos and energetic crisis.

Awaken Into Love

"If you knew your potential to feel good, you would ask no one to be different so that you can feel good. You would free yourself of all of that cumbersome impossibility of needing to control the world, or control your mate, or control your child. You are the only one who creates your reality. For no one else can think for you, no one else can do it. It is only you, every bit of it you." ~Esther Hicks

Journal

Bam, I found it.

My Trip To New York.

Last week I flew to New York City. For some people that would be no big deal, for others it's an "OMG, what fun." For me it was an "OMG, yuck." For a highly sensitive person, a big bustling city like New York can be a scary and exhausting place. I live in a rural area about 40 miles from downtown LA and I never like going there either. So it's nothing personal about New York City.

This trip was unique for my business and I couldn't get out of it.

I had two major worries:

 I would get stuck in an airport because this time of year major snow and ice storms go throughout the area almost every day.
 A long, six hour plane ride across the U.S. is uncomfortable (at times torture) for my body.

On top of those two concerns, I found out that I was on a red-eye arriving at 6 AM. Ugh. Added to that, I was only going to be there one day (trust me, I did not book this flight). How was I going to able to survive all of this so that I could do my job and thrive through it all?

Simple:
A- Investigate your destination.
B- Reframe the "ugh" to a positive adventure.

At first I did not know if I was going to get put up in a hotel or not. So I began looking for a hotel near JFK airport that I could stay at for an hourly rate so that I could at least freshen up and get a couple hours of sleep. FYI, a lot of hotels do this near busy airports for travelers who have long layovers or are snowbound. As I was looking, I got an email telling me that they got me a room already — in the heart of New York City. Thank you, Lord.
I investigated further and found that it was a quaint, historic hotel that was once owned by William Randolph Hearst for nearly a decade and many notables have chosen to live here ever since.

I find that historic places have a warm charm that new glass buildings will never have. The best news is that this hotel was only four blocks from Central Park and I wanted to experience it — BADLY.

The best place for highly sensitive people to get grounded and feel peaceful is in nature. And I figured that if I'm going all the way to New York on a red-eye and have to turn around and come back home the same day, then the least I can do for myself is to be in the world's greatest park.

The romantic side of me wanted to see the parts of the park that I've seen in romantic movies that I love, like *Maid In Manhattan* with Jennifer Lopez and Ralph Fiennes. I wanted to find the section of the park where she was walking with her son and the character Christopher Marshall, and where they sat down on a bench, surrounded with huge trees, in an expensive beautiful white coat that she borrowed from her unknowing hotel guest.

The second thing I wanted to experience was the amazing iconic Bethesda Fountain. You know, the one with the huge angel on the top.

I planned it all out and figured that I had the time to do this if I only napped for three hours after arriving. And hopefully, I would get some sleep on the flight over. My husband always loads a few movies onto my iPad so I can occupy the time and I always take noise canceling headphones to drown out the excess plane noise. (See the chapter on Travel for more ideas.)

Fast forward to me waking up in my hotel room from my nap — GROGGY. I began to go through a list in my head of why I should NOT go to Central park.

My body was saying go back to sleep.
My head was stuffed up.
It was drizzling outside.
I will get cold; there is snow everywhere.

I'm going to get all wet.
My only pair of shoes will get soaked.
I will have to wear wet shoes all the way home.
I'm hungry.
I could get mugged.

The list goes on, BUT the one thing that kept coming up was the reason TO go to the park. REGRET. The regret I would feel, going home, if I did not step outside of my comfort zone and explore the one place I had always wanted to see. I would regret it, forever.

Reframing

So I did what I teach all my clients — reframe the experience.
Briefly reframing is where you look at the past or future experience differently. Ask yourself questions like, "What else could this mean?" or "What if I have an amazing time?" or "What would I miss out on if I didn't do it?"

Now my NEW list in my head looked like this;
My body is not in charge of me.
My head will not fall off.
I have an umbrella.
The weather report says the rain will not get worse.

I brought New York snow clothes.
Wet shoes are a reminder of the great adventure.
I will eat before I leave.
I'm not going down dark alleys. (I also hid my wedding ring and ID.)

Bam, I found it.

When I texted my husband, he texted back, "What, the meaning of life?"

The title of this is not a reference to finding New York. It's that I eventually found the section of the park that had the benches that Jennifer Lopez sat on in her movie. You see, it was easy to find the Bethesda Fountain; all I had to do was ask someone. But how do you explain a specific, large, tree lined walkway with benches when the whole park is like that?
Not only did I find both of those, I also had the amazing, calming experience of being in the most breathtaking piece of nature nestled inside a huge bustling city. Totally worth being outside my comfort zone for.

This whole experience gave me such a level of certainty that I have the power to shape my day any way I want just by looking at it differently. A week later, I am still jazzed from my successful journey to Central Park.

A little side note: On the way to JFK to catch my flight home, traffic was so bad it took over an hour and a half and I missed my flight. This was the first time I have ever missed a flight.
I could have been stressed; my taxi driver was, but when I realized there was nothing we could do, I sat back and enjoyed the ride. The driver felt so bad he refused my tip, but I made him take it; it was not his fault. I'd like to think it helped him have a better day.

Fortunately, I was able to catch the next flight out and was able to slow down enough to get dinner beforehand.

By the way, when I got home, my husband told me that the ONE day that I was enjoying New York was the best weather New York has seen since January (this is March) and that a new storm closed all the airports the next morning.

I am one blessed and lucky girl.

Journal
What's in your life that you can reframe?

Journal
More about that...

The Importance of Nutrition and Wellness

If you are an HSP, then you are also more aware of when your body is not comfortable. Since HSPs are more sensitive to pain than most people, we work at being the most comfortable that we can be in every environment. Therefore, it is important to look at our health and wellness as a way to avoid overstimulation, exhaustion, and physical pain.

Sticking to simple foods that are full of nutrients and have a healthy balance are essential. Get the supplemental nutrients that our food no longer provides that will fully absorb into your system.

You also have to connect to nature and do regular exercise, relaxation, meditation, and any other activities that go with your nature to calm yourself down and recharge after the over-stimulation.

Functional Blood Test

One of the first things I do when I begin working with an HSP is to find out their general health. After only a few questions, I begin to see a pattern of unhealthy behavior regarding the person's daily practice of taking care of their health.

I can't quite remember when I first started studying natural medicine. I think it was about the time after I turned 50 and was researching natural hormone therapy while I was going through menopause. I was getting horrible migraines that could not be explained. I ended up changing my diet and using bio-identical hormones for about 18 months. It really made a difference while my body adjusted to my new life. Life went well for me for about five years until I began experiencing severe back pain. I attributed it to my profession of being a hairstylist at the time, being on my feet and leaning over people all day.

I saw my chiropractor for adjustments and got massages, but these were only temporary fixes until I began to look at the nutrients that my body needed. Once I began to take supplements that my body could use (instead of taking what would just go right through me), I was back to my happy self again.

The first thing I highly suggest is that you get a physical and some blood work. But not from your regular General Practitioner. You will get the most accurate picture of what your body is doing if you see a Board Certified Doctor in Integrative Medicine. These specialized doctors will order what is call a functional blood test. The results will show how your body is actually functioning — from your thyroid and organs to your hormones — and then you can get targeted healing treatments just for you.

This is how Dr. Corey King, a Board Certified Doctor in Integrative Medicine, explains laboratory ranges versus functional ranges:

Lab ranges come from the population that goes into the lab. If you think about the people that normally get blood work drawn, they are mainly the sick population. Yes, some healthy individuals do get blood work drawn, but it is mainly the sick patients going to the labs.

This is why the lab ranges are bell curves: Unless you are at the extreme high, or the extreme low, the doctors tell you, "Your blood tests look NORMAL!" However, you can still be sick and fall within their "normal" range, because the ranges are rather wide.

I call the functional ranges the "healthy ranges." They are tighter ranges when compared to the laboratory ranges. If you are outside of the functional ranges, then that will explain symptoms, but your doctors are not looking at the data because the data does not fall outside of their bell curve (aka laboratory ranges).

Also, if you fall outside of the laboratory ranges, this means you are either going to have surgery or be prescribed a medication.

If you are outside of the functional ranges, the doctors don't really care because they don't work with patients in regard to supplementation or nutrition; it is not their training.

My back finally said enough is enough.

In December 2010, about six months after marrying Michael, we went to a local amusement park and rode every ride like little kids. Two days later, I was cranky and in pain but didn't know that what was about to happen would change my life forever. The pain got progressively worse until I literally couldn't move. I had to be carried to the car and when I got to the doctor's office, I had to be carried in. The X-ray made me cry even more. Apparently, the curve in my spine had gotten progressively worse over the years to the point that it is now moderate scoliosis. The good news was that I had a strong, healthy system so I would be back on my feet in no time.

It was no picnic in the park. Because of the pinched nerve and compressed disc, I needed to get spinal decompression several times a week for a couple of months. But that was far better than surgery.

Fast forward two years later. Even though my back had healed, I still had to be very careful to not do too much. I wore a brace to work and needed to rest a lot. I think the whole episode triggered my high sensitivity over the top. Things were at a point that I thought I was going crazy.

I was beginning to forget the simplest things and was having vertigo episodes so frequently that I couldn't walk across the room with holding onto furniture.

Meeting Dr. Corey King

The chiropractor that I was seeing suggested that I see a doctor that could do a functional blood test so that I could get on the supplements and the treatments that I needed to support my new medical issues.

I wouldn't be here today, writing this book for you, if I had not found Dr. Corey King, a Board Certified Doctor in Integrative Medicine. His practice specializes in chronic conditions (listed in sources).

Lo and behold, not only was my thyroid out of whack, but my adrenal system had also gone into overdrive. Apparently, when my back went out, my whole system went into shock. My adrenal system went into fight or flight mode and had forgotten how to shut off. All of this affected my thyroid and digestive system. There was also a whole list of other stuff going on that attributed to my vertigo, things that I won't go into here.

After working with Dr. King, I now know how to take

care of my health simply by eating correctly and getting the nutritional support that my body needs.

Relax, Restore, and Revive Your Mind And Body

One of the tools I have found that helps a highly sensitive person is an Epsom salt water soak. You can do this in your own bathtub, but I found an amazing resource right in Dr. Kings office: **Float Spot**. At first I was skeptical yet intrigued about the reviews and the proven science of the benefits. And after I tried it, I was hooked.

This is an excerpt from Dr. King directly from the web page at http://floatspot.com/.

I have recently incorporated floating into my Integrative Medicine Clinic (Tustin Chronic Condition Center). Patients with a chronic health condition can greatly benefit from routine floating for several reasons: It helps to recover from stress, increases blood flow to all tissues, increases endorphin release, decreases muscle and joint soreness, decreases anxiety, detoxifies the body, and helps the adrenals glands to heal.

Adrenal gland function is critical for optimal health, and healing the adrenal glands is one positive aspect of floating. One hour of floating is equivalent to approximately four to five hours of sleep.
Looking at floating from a medical standpoint, this means that your adrenal glands (your stress glands: chemical, emotional, and physical) will heal and recover more quickly.

A majority of chronically sick patients that I see in my clinic have adrenal fatigue or failure, and for these patients, this is their Achilles heel! Without the adrenal glands' ability to recover, the chronically sick patient can suffer from thyroid gland dysfunction, weight gain, brain fog, gastro intestinal discomfort, and insomnia. I highly recommend anyone suffering with a chronic health condition to add regular floating into their weekly routine, to speed up metabolic and neurological recovery.

USANA Nutritional Program

I feel better

My purpose here is to not be a commercial but to share with you a little bit of why I have chosen to have USANA products as my nutritional support system.

The number one reason that I am using USANA products is that I feel better. *A lot better.*

About a year ago, a friend of mine, who has been using USANA for almost 20 years, suggested I try the 5-day RESET program. I wanted to lose some weight and she let me know that 4.5 pounds is the typical weight loss for this first five days. My own research about the program showed that it might also work on the sugar and carb cravings I was having and help to "kick start," cleanse, and prepare my body for further weight loss. To my surprise, I did lose five pounds in the first five days, and I stayed with the program for another loss of five pounds in the next month.

Even though I initially wanted to lose some weight, what I received as a benefit is worth its weight in gold. All those little aches and pains that I was constantly experiencing went away. *Coincidence?*

So I asked my friend, Karen, "What is the USANA difference?" The answer was very simple. USANA supplements are developed to dissolve in our stomachs within a timeframe based on pharmaceutical guidelines, and then to pass into the small intestine and bloodstream for transit to cells.
They are what is called "bioavailable." It shocked me to learn that there are no rules for dissolving time for vitamins. So most tablet vitamins are made to stay solid in storage, and they end up passing through our system – and out our "exit" – in the same solid state.

Even before this "bioavailability" factor, USANA's recipe for its multivitamins is based on the types and ratios of nutrients required to keep cells alive in culture. That is a hard feat for any scientist! If one nutrient is omitted, the cells die. So, not only was this list and ratio maintained for USANA's multivitamins, but their scientists added proper further ratios of antioxidants to the mix, carefully preserving balance, because we don't have the luxury of living in a stress-free lab dish!

Our hectic lifestyle can become a health risk, especially for an HSP. What may be a normal day for most people will overwhelm most HSP. In some careers, jobs, and even academic communities, there is a huge social demand to perform and succeed at the highest level.

Then there is social media, TV, movies, sports activities, and anything else that pushes and pulls at us to do more and more.

I will always be secretly and eternally grateful when my young boys decided that they did not want to play after school sports like their friends.

Life Like A Hermit?

Unless you decide to live the life of a hermit, you will

experience some stress in your life that could potentially cause health issues.

The food that is available to us to eat is especially troublesome. More and more GMO food is getting into our food supply and causing havoc with our health. My husband and I just saw a documentary on Netflix, *GMO OMG*, that questioned that very issue. HSP's bodies are especially vulnerable to the effects of toxins and pesticides. With USANA's help, I am able to support my cells.

USANA — off on the right foot

USANA has been around since 1992, so they're experienced (that's a plus).

Plus, they have substance to go along with their great looks. They've got top-notch manufacturing facilities, their own scientists and research and development team, and the highest standards for their nutritional products.
Plus, they have award-winning products. They don't like to brag, but they come pretty highly recommended.

That's because they got off on the right foot.
They were founded by a scientist—not a corporate suit.

USANA's founder, Dr. Myron Wentz, is an internationally recognized microbiologist, immunologist, and pioneer in infectious disease diagnosis. In 1974, he founded Gull Laboratories to develop viral diagnostics, and his greatest successes during this time included the first commercially available diagnostic test for Epstein-Barr virus, better known as the virus that causes mononucleosis.

But success was never Dr. Wentz's only aim. Instead, he centered his life around a dream of a world free from pain and suffering. A world free from disease. And he founded USANA to help further his dream by providing people all over the world with the most advanced supplements science can produce.

This is why USANA is a company based on continuous product innovation. This is why they have stringent manufacturing processes, ongoing scientific research, and an insatiable drive to produce exceptional products.

This is why USANA is trusted by over 700 professional athletes, Olympians, and also everyday people who believe health is a vital part of a long, happy life.
We all know that Olympians put their bodies through extremes. So they must feed their bodies in a way
that supports their dreams of winning. Plus, they cannot take even the smallest of a chance of being tested positive for any substance that would be

considered performance enhancements. USANA backs their products with a "Million Dollar Athlete Guarantee" that no athlete will test positive for banned substances from their consumption of USANA. That is why USANA is their number one choice.

What you just read is why I have chosen to not only be a customer of USANA but also to be a partner in this amazing company with the highest of standards.

If you would like more information about how you too can experience the benefits of USANA, check out the **Sources** page at the end of this book.

Egoscue Pain Free Centers

Being an HSP does not automatically mean you will experience the physical challenges and pain that some of us do. But if you are one of those that are sensitive to pain and want long lasting relief, here are some suggestions.

If you happen to have any painful physical challenges, I am highly suggesting that you find an Egoscue Pain Free Center near you and check them out. If you do not have one near you, they will work with you through the magic of your computer screen on Skype. You will not regret it.

At the writing of this book, it's now a little bit over four years after my back did a total blow out. And I do wonder, at times, if the highly sensitive emotional stress I experience has anything to do with my scoliosis getting worse.

Was my unchecked emotional pressure causing a physical pressure that in turn caused my spinal structure to curve enough to have a total collapse?
It's hard to equate that. All I know is that I got to a place in life where I decided that I MUST change and get control of my high sensitivity because what I was doing, up until then, was not working.

I know deep in my heart and soul that God has a plan for all of us. His plan for me is to show others who are in pain, emotional and physical, how they cannot just exist but thrive in our chaotic world. I can only believe that He wanted me to learn firsthand so that I could congruently serve others.

One day, in early January 2015, I finally decided to find an Egoscue Pain Free Center. I had experienced some pain relief a year ago when I had met an Egoscue therapist at a Tony Robbins event and she worked with me for a brief time.

Now I felt it was time to completely commit to a

program. To my surprise, there was a clinic 20 minutes from my house.

I want to introduce Chris Kussoff. He is the owner of the Egoscue Pain Free Center here in Laguna Hills, California. He graciously agreed to take time out of his busy schedule to write this excerpt, especially for this book, explaining how Egoscue therapy is so important, especially for Highly Sensitive People.

"In my 16 years as an Egoscue Practitioner, I have seen many profound changes in people. I have seen almost every symptom imaginable either decrease or go away completely.
The changes to a person's life that occur after that are equally profound. With the body aligned and the painful symptoms gone, the body has a whole new energy and life source. You now have energy to deal with life as it shows up.
No longer is the day of physical, mental, and emotional struggle. Your view of the world is not through the ache, pain, and sometimes hopeless view. It is fresh and alive."

Where Did Egoscue Come From?
Egoscue is a proprietary system of Postural Therapy developed by Pete Egoscue in 1971.

Pronounced E-gos-que and considered the World Leader in Non-Medical Pain Relief, this revolutionary method for stopping chronic pain is deeply rooted in the belief that your body is not broken, your design is not flawed, your posture is.

They've developed a program that is natural, makes sense, and gets results. It puts you back in the driver's seat of your health with a series of gentle corrective exercises, called E-Cises®, tailored exclusively for you. This custom therapeutic approach brings your posture back into balance, thus returning your body to proper function. You can expect to feel better, have less or no pain, restore your physical self-confidence, increase your daily energy, and just feel good again!

So how does it all go wrong?

The posture and alignment is dictated by the functionality of the muscular skeletal system. The posture is a stimulus based system. This means what you put into the system will have a cause and effect relationship.

Remember, the muscles move the bones. What if we tell the muscles each and every day to slouch, round, and get tight, as with a sitting job? As this stimulus accumulates in the body, it will create positional and structural change to the posture, eventually leading to pain and breakdown.

Looking At This From A HSP Angle

How is the body feeling as this process is occurring? As you can imagine, not too good. There is a significant negative stress growing and building in the body each day. This is especially true for a Highly Sensitive Person who has not yet learned how to prevent or let go of these daily stresses.
This will, of course, significantly affect your ability to deal with all the other stress in the world. The body has a functional limit to the amount of daily stress it can endure. If your limit has been nearly reached by your structural compensations alone, you have a hard time dealing with the world. - Chris Kussoff

A Series Of Gentle Corrective Exercises

Gentle, corrective exercises are exactly what an HSP needs to be able to feel relief, get centered, and be in control. I have found that the E-Cises® are similar to yoga, with the added benefit of correcting my posture and easing my physical pain.

Real Science, Real Results

One of the traits of a Highly Sensitive Person is the high need to feel good at all times. An unhappy HSP will go to great lengths to try to feel better when their world is in chaos. And part of that is looking great. That is why some of our greatest clothing designers are HSP. Not to mention makeup artists, skin care professionals, and hair stylists.

In all my years of being a Cosmetologist, I never noticed that my most difficult clients were also unresourceful HSPs.

What I mean by unresourceful is that they always expected me to be able to make them feel better by making them look better. And I was pretty good at doing that for about six weeks. Then their hair grew out and they came back in grumpy again. As a result of this, I would always look for and suggest a hair or skin care product that would give them a long term beautiful effect until their next appointment. They would try almost anything that I suggested. I felt like a hero with these clients even though they exhausted me.

Over the years, as I got older, so did my clients and soon they were asking me for something to get rid of the wrinkles that were creeping in. They wanted to know what I was doing to look 10+ years younger. As a licensed Cosmetologist, I am also trained in skin care so they knew I had the answers.

Until recently, I was only able to refer them to have a facial, buy an expensive skin care system, or see a plastic surgeon. Now I can offer NeriumAD™.

A single product that delivers superior results

Prior to joining Nerium International, Amber Olson owned and operated a medical spa: *"All of the products that we sold were essentially the same ingredients in different packages. NeriumAD™ contains a groundbreaking new ingredient, allowing our product to truly sell itself."*

She goes on to say, *"Our customers previously had to use four to five different products to achieve anything close to these results. We can now give them a single night cream that can deliver the best results they've ever had in improving discoloration, reducing the appearance of wrinkles, and fighting the signs of aging."*

NeriumAD™ skincare products are formulated to improve the appearance of:
- Fine lines and wrinkles
- Discoloration
- Uneven skin tone
- Enlarged pores
- Sagging skin

When I was introduced to NeriumAD™ by my friend, I was skeptical. After being in the beauty industry for over 20 years, I knew more about skin than the average person. But when I saw how her skin had improved, I got curious AND she was going to let me try it for free. I figured that the only thing I had to lose was my wrinkles.

Within a week I began to experience my skin being softer, and in a short period of time I began to notice an improvement in the tone and fine lines around my eyes and mouth. My highly sensitive skin loved it. NeriumAD™ makes me excited when I see my reflection. I now instantly smile looking in the mirror. The best thing is that I got to stop using foundation makeup. As a HSP, most of us do not like heavy lotions and creams on our skin.

Never have I seen a product work like this. Bonus: It is super easy to use. One product, at night, done. I was hooked. My husband, Michael, is also using it because it reduces the irritation from his shaving and it is so simple to use (men love simple).

After almost a year of using the product, I realized that I was recommending it to my HSP clients, family, and friends to the point that all I was hearing was how amazing it made them feel.
That was when I began to do my own research about the company. What I found out blew me and my husband away. Long story short, we decided to

partner with Nerium International and are now Independent Brand Partners.

Below are statements from real users:

"My skin is SO sensitive, and I hated using anything on it. I used the product, and I couldn't believe the results! It's the best feeling in the world!" – RJ, CA

"I've never really gotten into a routine of washing my face at night, but now I look forward to it, because I know I'm about to apply a healthy dose of Nerium. Love it!" – Padriac, AZ

"I am always looking for a product with real results. I love the results I am seeing with Nerium, and others are seeing it as well." – Penny, SC

"So it's now Day 14 of my Nerium Experience and here's what I'm seeing: smaller pores and less redness." – Lara, TX

"Nerium is awesome. My face is looking the best it has looked in years. It has helped with my skin problems. My pores are looking better, too." – Evelyn, TX

If you would like more information about how you too can experience the benefits of NeriumAD, check out the **Sources** page at the end of this book.

My hope as you are reading this information is that you begin to understand the importance of taking care of any physical and/or emotional pain that you might be experiencing and seek out the help that best serves you.

Be Your Own Health Advocate

The reason I told you my story was for you to understand how important it is to listen to your body and keep searching for the specific help you need for whatever health issues you may have. Don't let anyone tell the highly sensitive side of you that you're crazy for what you know is true.
We are so fortunate to have an abundance of choices in the medical field today; whether it's natural or not, you owe it to yourself to have an amazing, pain-free, healthy life.

It's important to stay grounded by:
- Getting a lot of sleep (eight hours minimum, sometimes more)
- Exercising daily, preferably outside, to calm your nervous system and clear your mind

- Eating healthy food
- During your quiet alone time, reading books, listening to soothing music, and journal writing

- Whenever you need to be alone, finding a quiet place where you can be alone.
- Investing time and energy only in friendships that are good for you, people who accept you for who you are and support you in the way that you live.

Now is the time to take stock of your own health and wellness. Most of us HSPs will keep busy, take a drug, eat when we're not hungry, or have a glass of wine to distract us from what we are feeling, be it emotional or physical pain.

I urge you to take a moment of really getting real with yourself, right now, and say ENOUGH is ENOUGH.
 "I will no longer tolerate the low standards I have for my health and well-being. I am worth it to be the very best version of myself so that I can live a life that is wonderful, thriving and rich with purpose."

In the end, what I can now say is that I feel really healthy and look more than ten years younger for the first time in over five years.

I have committed to feeling and looking great with daily Egoscue therapies, USANA Nutrition, and Nerium Anti-aging products for the rest of my life.

Journal
Go ahead and journal what you are going to commit to about your health...

Chapter Four

Your Faith, God NEVER wastes a pain

Believing in something greater than you.

I wanted to add this chapter because I feel that it is important for you to see what the possibility of peace and joy is when you know when your deep feelings are supported.

When I was a little girl, I always had a unique connection with my father. If I could guess, he was probably an HSP too. I wasn't actually aware that this was unique within my family until, as an adult, I learned how to tap into my deeper feelings about joy and happiness — plus, my Aunt Mary, my father's sister, asked me one day, "Didn't you know you were your dad's favorite?"

When I was about 11 years old, I experienced a powerful event when, of all things, I was fishing with my father. This experience did not have an immediate, conscious impact on me. Yet years later, when I was in my late 40s, it came back to me as I was being coached by a friend helping me to find my inner peace. All he asked me was to remember a time where I was truly happy and, boom, this memory came flooding back.

My dad loved fishing and would occasionally take me with him. I wasn't particularly excited about fishing, but I loved being with my dad whenever I could. He was one of the few people in my life that I felt completely safe with. He enjoyed me being me. So there we were at the edge of a small canal of water where there were usually plenty of catfish. My dad baited the hook and dropped the line in the water. I have no memory of how long we waited; all I know is that I soon felt a tug on the line and screamed with delight.

My dad rescued me by helping me pull the fish up.

 At that moment, I looked up into his eyes and saw the most powerful light of love, happiness, and joy, and I experienced a connection so deep in my heart and soul that I can only explain it as God coming through my dad for me. In that brief moment, my dad disappeared and all I knew was pure love embracing every cell of my body.

Years later, my dad sent me a note where he wrote, *Jesus says he loves you*. I truly believe that my dad was blessed by God and was here for us to know God and Jesus through him. He is in Heaven now; I am sure of it.

Daily Exercises About Spiritual Life

One of the many books I have read to help myself and other Highly Sensitive People is *The Highly Sensitive Person's Companion: Daily Exercises for Calming Your Senses in an Over stimulating World*, authored by Ted Zeff, PhD.

Reprising his successful first book, *The Highly Sensitive Person's Survival Guide*, author Ted Zeff offers new daily practices and skill-building exercises to help you survive in our over-stimulating world, and shares many thoughtful insights and solutions to problems for highly sensitive people.

This is an excerpt from "Daily Exercises about Spiritual Life."

"A Spiritual Life Calms the HSP"

One of the best attributes of being an HSP is your inherent capacity to have deep spiritual experiences. In this final section of the book, we are going to discuss ways to develop your spiritual connection with the divine, which will bring you inner peace.

The more you develop your sense of spirituality, the easier it will be to cope with daily overstimulation. Some of us may have a resistance to pursuing a spiritual path due to early negative religious experiences.

You may want to think of spirituality in terms of unconditional love, beauty in nature, or Higher Power. You may also be more comfortable relating spiritually to a specific deity or teacher like Christ, Buddha, or Krishna, or to a prophet like Abraham, Mohammed, or Moses. I know one person who is an agnostic but acknowledges that there is a mystery to life when he considers the vastness and the order of the universe.

Transcendence Through Spiritual Practices

Essentially all religions teach the same thing — to love the divine Higher Power and to be compassionate to others and yourself. The more we can take comfort in the divine presence within, the better able we will be to cope with life's challenges. The stable, unwavering love of God gives us succor during stressful times.

Spend some time thinking about your spiritual orientation as an HSP. Write down some examples of how your attainment to the divine have helped you during challenging times. How can your spiritual practices help you with a current challenge?

Some examples are:

*Whenever I feel the peace of God in nature, watching a beautiful sunset, looking at the vastness of the universe on a clear starry night, my job worries become insignificant.

*Instead of being upset about my divorce, I close my eyes and focus on my inner body, feeling divine energy flowing through me until I become peaceful.

*When I get angry at my partner, I inwardly ask, "Who is getting hurt?" When I realize that it's the temporarily hurt ego that's upset and that I'm so much more than just the angry thoughts arising in my mind, I'm able to release the anger.

*I pray deeply for my mother's health to improve and then after I experience a profound divine connection, I feel that God's will is done regardless of the outcome.

*When I accept a challenging situation in the present moment instead of wishing that things were different, I know that everything happens in a divine right order."

End of excerpt.

Pray Differently

Practice Giving Thanks To God For All That Is Good

As a Christian Counselor, I see people deeply hurting and used to always wonder why God has not answered their prayers.

People think that they need to keep praying more. More is not a bad idea, but what if you prayed different?

Could it be as easy as talking to your Father? Simple yet difficult.

Solutions come from all types of sources. When I was taking a course in public speaking, we were taught to evaluate the other students with a feedback sandwich. This is a way of giving feedback that the student will take in and learn from and not reject. It's been proven to escalate the learning process tenfold.

It is in three parts, just like a sandwich:

First, say what was great about it, what you appreciated, and what you're grateful for.
Then say what needs improvement on, your request for what you want.
Then finish up with an overall thank you and graciousness. Through Jesus name, Amen.

Can you see how God would hear your prayer better when you're grateful for what He has already given you? And the belief that all things through Jesus are possible is why God gave him to us in the first place.

Through the process of counseling, I help people see and know that:
- With God they are capable in all things.
- God's delay is not God's denial.
- Sometimes our Heavenly Father says yes, sometimes he says no, and sometimes he says not yet.
- We can also experience God's amazing sense of humor on a daily basis.
- He will always give us what we need, not what we want.
- He gives us life experiences and challenges because he loves us and wants us to grow and be closer to him.* God has your back.
- Life doesn't happen to you; it happens for you.
- God NEVER wastes a pain.

Jesus Calling

This is an excerpt from the book *Jesus Calling*, by Sarah Young.

"As you sit quietly in My presence, let Me fill your heart and mind with thankfulness. This is the most direct way to achieve a thankful stance. If your mind needs a focal point, gaze at My Love poured out for you on the cross. Remember that nothing in heaven or on earth can separate you from that Love. This remembrance builds a foundation that circumstances cannot shake.

As you go through this day, look for tiny treasures strategically placed along the way. Lovingly go before you and plant little pleasures to brighten your day. Look carefully for them, pluck them one by one. When you reach the end of the day, you will have gathered a lovely bouquet. Offer it up to Me with a grateful heart. Receive My Peace as you lie down to sleep, with thankful thoughts playing a lullaby in your mind." Romans 8:38-39; Psalm 4:7-8

Our lives are much richer and more fulfilling when we contribute to others in a way that enhances their lives too. Think of all the people in your life that have been mentors to you throughout their painful trials and tribulations, unafraid to tell their personal story of tragedy and pain so that you could hear courage, bravery, humbleness, and honesty.

There is something deep inside all of us that yearns to break free from the pain that holds us back. How can we use our highly sensitive abilities to enjoy life and serve the highest good of others and God? What if we could take all that pain and use it, release it, break free from it? Just imagine what life would be like for you and all the people you touch.

Your mission, if you choose to accept it, is to embrace your pain, not try to get rid of it.

Use your pain to drive you to help yourself so that you can help others.
When I was at the most painful time of my journey and all I saw was obstacles, I kept asking myself one question, "If I can't do that, what can I do?" That is how the concept of this book was born.

Journal Writing System

Author Pastor Rick Warren, Saddleback Church

"I will climb my watchtower and wait to see what the LORD will tell me to say and what answer he will give to my complaint. The LORD gave me this answer: 'Write down clearly on tablets what I reveal to you.'" (Habakkuk 2:1-2 TEV)

Because Habakkuk wrote down what the Lord said to him, we have the book called Habakkuk. Because

David wrote down what God spoke to him, we have the book of Psalms. They asked God a question, God gave them an answer, and they wrote it down.

If your prayer life is stuck in a rut and you feel like you're saying the same prayers over and over, one of the best things you can do is start writing down your prayers. It makes it more personal, and it helps you be more serious about your prayers.

This is called the spiritual habit of journaling. It's a habit that will help you refresh your prayer life. But don't make it too complicated! Simply write down what you're saying to God, and write down what God's saying to you.
After you get your notebook, remember these two practical suggestions to help make your journaling more effective.

First, put a vertical line down the center of the page.

On one side, write what you say to God. On the other side, write what God says to you. As you write down what you say to God, don't expect him to always say something to you immediately. Sometimes he'll answer later in the day, or he may even wake you up in the middle of the night.

Then, on the same sheet of paper, draw a horizontal line.

Above the line, write "Yesterday" and record the events of your day. Underneath the line, write "Life Lessons." The next day, look back on the events of the day before and ask, "What lesson was God trying to teach me through those events?" God is trying to teach us lessons through the everyday events of our lives, but we miss them all the time. When you take time to write them out in this way, it will help you focus on hearing God's voice and what he wants you to learn from him.
Journaling is a very powerful habit. It helps you focus your thoughts.
It helps you remember what you said and what God said. It helps you test the impressions that you get from God.

It also helps you worship as you thank God for speaking to you.

"O Lord, now I have heard your report, and I worship you in awe." (Habakkuk 3:2 TLB)

Journal
Try It Yourself

Less Is More

Let go so that something greater, more precious and fulfilling will be part of your life.

This next story reminds me of a time in early 2009 when I had just moved into a temporary home. I knew that I was only going to be there for a few months so to save time and energy, I only unpacked what was absolutely necessary to be comfortable with.

After about a week of settling in, I sat down one night to relax with my cup of tea and my little dog, Marcel, and began to notice how freeing and peaceful I felt.

Looking around the room, I asked myself a deep question, "What about this is so peaceful?" The answer came quickly. It was that I didn't have extra stuff, not even a picture on the wall that "chattered" at me.

One of the traits of being an HSP is that we see more deeply than other people. Colors, shapes, and textures can profoundly move us as if they are talking to us. On one hand we enjoy it, but on the other it can be exhausting and stressful if there is too much stimulation going on.

Journal
Can you remember a time when you didn't have a lot of "stuff" chattering at you?

My hope is that you enjoy this beautiful story and journal about what you could clean up and let go of in order to have more. Because sometimes less is more.

The Pearl Necklace

The cheerful girl with bouncy golden curls was almost five. Waiting with her mother at the checkout stand, she saw them: a circle of glistening white pearls in a pink foil box.

"Oh please, Mommy. Can I have them? Please, Mommy, please!"

Quickly, the mother checked the back of the little foil box and then looked back into the pleading blue eyes of her little girl's upturned face.

"A dollar ninety-five. That's almost $2.00. If you really want them, I'll think of some extra chores for you and in no time you can save enough money to buy them for yourself. Your birthday's only a week away and you might get another crisp dollar bill from Grandma."

As soon as Jenny got home, she emptied her penny bank and counted out 17 pennies. After dinner, she did more than her share of chores and she went to the neighbor and asked Mrs. McJames if she could pick dandelions for ten cents.

On her birthday, Grandma did give her another new dollar bill and at last she had enough money to buy the necklace.

Jenny loved her pearls. They made her feel dressed up and grown up. She wore them everywhere-- Sunday school, kindergarten, even to bed. The only time she took them off was when she went swimming or had a bubble bath. Mother said if they got wet, they might turn her neck green.

Jenny had a very loving daddy and every night when she was ready for bed, he would stop whatever he was doing and come upstairs to read her a story. One night when he finished the story, he asked Jenny, "Do you love me?"

"Oh yes, Daddy. You know that I love you."

"Then give me your pearls."

"Oh, Daddy, not my pearls. But you can have Princess — the white horse from my collection. The one with the pink tail. Remember, Daddy? The one you gave me. She's my favorite."

"That's okay, Honey. Daddy loves you. Good night." And he brushed her cheek with a kiss.

About a week later, after the story time, Jenny's daddy asked again, "Do you love me?"

"Daddy, you know I love you."

"Then give me your pearls."

"Oh Daddy, not my pearls. But you can have my baby doll. The brand new one I got for my birthday. She is so beautiful and you can have the yellow blanket that matches her sleeper."

"That's okay. Sleep well. God bless you, little one. Daddy loves you." And as always, he brushed her cheek with a gentle kiss.

A few nights later when her daddy came in, Jenny was sitting on her bed with her legs crossed Indian-style. As he came close, he noticed her chin was trembling and one silent tear rolled down her cheek.

"What is it, Jenny? What's the matter?"

Jenny didn't say anything but lifted her little hand up to her daddy. And when she opened it, there was her little pearl necklace. With a little quiver, she finally said, "Here, Daddy. It's for you."

With tears gathering in his own eyes, Jenny's kind daddy reached out with one hand to take the dime-store necklace, and with the other hand he reached into his pocket and pulled out a blue velvet case with a strand of genuine pearls and gave them to Jenny.

He had them all the time. He was just waiting for her to give up the dime-store stuff so he could give her genuine treasure.

—Author unknown

Journal
What are you hanging on to that if you let it go of it, you would experience a greater joy?

Chapter Five

"It won't be as good as I hope, and it's not as bad as I am making it."

Solutions

There are as many solutions to an HSP's life challenges as there are stars in the sky.

The good news is that there are many to choose from and you might even be surprised when you find something that works for you that is not even here in this book.

Some of you may try everything that you see here plus try advice from others and still not resolve the chaotic challenges you are having.

That is exactly why I professionally coach Highly Sensitive People to help them tap into their potential and get them out of crisis and chaos so that they will have a Wonderful Life.

It's your Life, let's make it Wonderful.

Powerful Questions

The one gift that HSPs have is the ability to be deep thinkers. And you can use this ability to be able to make a huge positive difference in not only your life but other's lives as well.

The most powerful way to do that is to ask yourself deep questions.
My friend Tony Robbins always says, *"If you want better answers, ask better questions."*

Here is a powerful way to not only set up your day for success but to also finish it so that you get a better night's sleep.

Morning Activation Questions

Priming Yourself To Have An Amazing Day

- What am I most happy about in my life right now? What makes me happy? How does that make me feel?
- What am I excited about in my life right now? What makes me excited? How does that make me feel?

- What am I proud of in my life right now? What about that makes me proud? How does that make me feel?

- What am I grateful for in my life right now? What about that makes me grateful? How does that make me feel?

- What am I enjoying most in my life right now? What about that do I enjoy? How does that make me feel?

- What am I committed to in my life right now? What about that makes me committed? How does that make me feel?

- Who do I love? Who loves me? What about them makes me loving? How does that make me feel?

Evening Calming Questions

Relief So You Can Sleep

- What have I given today? In what ways have I been a giver today?

- What did I learn today?

- How has today added to the quality of my life? How can I use today as an investment in my future?

Additional Success Questions

- Did I give — Am I giving my full effort?
- How can I give my full effort now?
- If I were to give my full effort, what would happen?

- Did I learn — Am I learning something?
- How can I begin to learn something now?
- If I begin learning now, what will happen?

"I pray that your heart will be flooded with light so that you can see something of the future that God has called you to share." —Ephesians 1:18

Journal
Your Answers To The Questions

Journal
More Space for more answers

Inner or Outer Energy?

Here is something that I found works for many people:

I first ask, "Where are you feeling the energy? Inside your body or outside your body?" If it's inside, I walk them through a visualization of helping someone do something fun, baking cookies, shopping, walking in a park or on the beach.

If the answer is it's outside the body, then I help them get in touch with themselves. They have lost the connection with their inner being and need to get it back. After we are with people, we tend to let them be our boundaries. Sitting quietly and listening to your breath, doing some form of quiet movements, meditation, or yoga all can help.

What if you could decide to make your sensitivity your best friend? What would you do for your best friend? Be understanding, patient, and loyal, supporting it through thick and thin?

Most of us are very visual and tactile and get grounded in nature. So I like to have thriving plants, natural stones, sea shells, and pretty objects around for me to touch and see.
   I keep small polished stones and shells in easy reach on my desk.

Something that most people don't know about me, until now, is that I am a Lego geek. I find that creating something with Legos is very balancing. The activity uses both the left and right sides of your brain at the same time.

I also must share with you an activity that not only brings great joy, it also is very relaxing for me and also other creative HSPs: highly detailed Coloring books by Sue Coccia. Check them out at www.earthartinternational.com. There are a multitude of these types of books on Amazon. I like Sue's art the best.

Keeping a diary and/or journaling is one of my best resources. It can be as simple as jotting down any thoughts as they come to you throughout the day, or it can be a system like the one I shared in the chapter titled "Your Faith." Below is a quick recap.

This is called the "spiritual habit of journaling." It's a habit that will help you refresh your prayer life. But don't make it too complicated! Simply write down what you're saying to God, or any other source of spirit that inspires you, and write down what God, or source, is saying to you.

Remember these two practical suggestions to help make your journaling more effective.

First, put a vertical line down the center of the page.
On one side, write what you say to God. On the other side, write what God says to you. As you write down what you say to God, don't expect him to always say something to you immediately. Sometimes he'll answer later in the day, or he may even wake you up in the middle of the night.

Then, on the same sheet of paper, draw a horizontal line.

Above the line, write "Yesterday" and record the events of your day. Underneath the line, write "Life Lessons." The next day, look back on the events of the day before and ask, "What lesson was God trying to teach me through those events?" God is trying to teach us lessons through the everyday events of our lives, but we miss them all the time. When you take time to write them out in this way, it will help you focus on hearing God's voice and what he wants you to learn from him.

Journaling is a very powerful habit. It helps you focus your thoughts. It helps you remember what you said and what God said. It helps you test the impressions that you get from God.

I can list out a lot more ideas that I have picked up from other HSPs, but the best source that I have found is a workbook written by Dr. Elaine Aron, "The Highly Sensitive Person's Workbook."

Journal

HSP Traveling

I love to travel. About every six weeks I am flying for business and/or fun, because I have the traits of not only an HSP but also fall into the category of being a HSS, High Sensation Seeker. I attribute it to the fact that my family moved a lot when I was a child. If you think you might be an HSS, you can go to Elaine Aron's website at http://hsperson.com/test/high-sensation-seeking-test/ to take a self-evaluation.

A couple of years ago, one of my clients, for whom I travel, put me up in a "spa type hotel" and I was hooked. I don't know how many spa type hotels there are around, but I know of a great one in Palm Beach, Florida. A lot of times they are referred to as *Boutique Style Hotels*. After a long flight across the U.S., plus working, this has become the perfect refuge before I head back home.

Traveling With Other People

When I fly with my husband, it can be challenging in a different way. He wants to hurry up and get settled at the gate. And he worries about every little thing that could possibly go wrong. In one sense, this trait is needed as long as he can use it to be prepared before we even leave home. Yet, when his uncertainty shows up as soon as we enter the airport parking lot, that's a problem for me.

I learned a long time ago that no matter how much you try to prepare, something might happen to derail your best laid plans and you need to just go with the flow. God has a sense of humor, is what I say.

So before each and every trip, I remind my husband of what I need so that I am happy.

Navigating An Airport

The biggest things that will help you the most when you are in a huge (they're all huge) airport that you are not familiar with is to:

- Get there early. Plan for two hours before your flight.
- If you're checking bags, see if your airline has curbside service.
- Stop and get your bearings.
- Get through TSA security.
- Stop and put yourself together.
- Find the flight status monitor so you can see what gate your flight is at.
- Find what direction you need to start walking in.
- Look ahead and see what path you need to take with the least amount of people in the way. The path of least resistance.

- Along the way, stop and use the restroom.
- Buy a bottle of water and maybe some food. I always pack my own food and snacks.

It sounds simple, yet it can be difficult if the person you're traveling with just wants to GO and figure things out along the way. That will only add to my heightened sense of the jumbled mess of a big airport with thousands of anxious people trying to get somewhere.

When I travel, I have found that earplugs work great but noise canceling headphones are even better.

I have also purchased TSA pre-check. That way I can get through the airport security line quicker and don't have to go through all the challenges of unpacking and packing back up again.

Another travel recovery solution is the Float Spot that I mentioned in the Health and Wellness chapter. One session can help jet lag. Research shows that floating in a float tank is much more effective than bed rest. Visit http://floatspot.com/.

My Honeymoon

I clearly remember our honeymoon almost five years ago. It was a beautiful seven day Caribbean cruise on the largest ship on the planet, the Oasis. We live in California and needed to fly to Florida to finally catch the ship. This was the very first time we had traveled together over an extended period of time. And it was before I discovered that I had extreme HSP abilities.

My husband practically planned the whole trip and I was actually grateful for that. He is way more detail-oriented than I am and this is one time that this valuable trait is much needed.

He wanted to make the trip very special for both of us.

He rented a Limo to take us to the airport and pick us up when we returned. This was important as we needed to fly from and back to LAX, which is an hour away from where we live. Michael also surprised me with first class seats on the flight.

We arrived at the airport in plenty of time and well rested, and flew to Florida early enough to rent a car and take a ride on a boat into the Florida Everglades and still get on the ship in time.

The ship is the most beautiful ship I've ever seen, with amenities you'd never believe. It even has a central park with over 2000 trees and plants. This was a dream come true. The art throughout the ship is breathtaking and I was in heaven.

Everywhere on the ship there were people that wanted to take care of our every whim. So why I was constantly fatigued during the whole trip? I felt like I was missing out on most of the enjoyment of the trip and just wanted to stay in our cabin and rest. Don't get me wrong, we did have fun — the pictures we took are evidence. But I felt that I was always unsettled, which for an HSP is exhausting.

We also did not account for the extreme heat and humidity, especially in St. Marten. I felt I was melting like butter on a hot sidewalk. I have never tolerated heat well and this was the worst ever. We found a French bakery where Michael drooled over pastries and croissants, yet all I wanted was the ice cold bottled water. We ended up on China Beach, our destination, and even though it was raining, I immediately ran into the ocean. Awe. Saved.

Why I Was Overwhelmed

Each and every day I was taking in all of the newness, beauty, and excitement that surrounded us and I was not letting it go. I gathered all the pieces and the moments of the day in an imaginary basket until it was overflowing and I couldn't get one more thing in. This I carried with me all day. It quickly got so heavy that I no longer had any energy for anything.

I also was acutely aware that I wanted to please my new husband and just blindly did whatever he wanted to do.

Now that I look back on it, with the knowledge that I now have about my HSP ability and what I MUST do to take care of myself, I know why I was overwhelmed and what I will do on future trips.

The Unique HSP

Every Highly Sensitive Person is unique, with unique needs. We are all different and as unique as our fingerprints.

Here's what I have learned to do when I travel, my list of highly recommended items for successful HSP travel:
- Earplugs
- Noise canceling headphones
- Sunglasses
- Hat
- Hand sanitizer

- Surface sanitizer wipes (The first thing I do when I sit down in my airplane seat is to wipe down EVERYTHING that any previous passengers have touched or sneezed on.)
- Small fanny pack or cross body purse for all your travel documents and money
- iPad or similar device to watch a movie. It will distract you from air turbulence

Here are some of the things I do at the airport to ensure successful HSP travel:
- I arrive at the airport early.
- After getting through security, I purchase water and any food I might want.
- I travel frequently enough that I purchased TSA Pre-check so I can get through security easier and faster. It eliminates having to put myself back together.

If you don't have TSA Pre-check, then find a bench or chair to put yourself together before you move on.

If you're expecting to be in a warm environment, make sure you are prepared with a wet neck towel and drinking water. I personally have no problem pouring my drinking water on my head to cool off.

The same goes for cold weather. Pack extra socks and layer up with your clothes.

Make downtime a MUST. No matter where you are,

you can always pull your hat over your eyes, put on your sunglasses and your ear plugs, and sit in a quiet corner.

Research your trip. Make sure that the people you're traveling with understand your needs and your plans that serve you. A noisy bar late at night for dancing and drinking may not be your thing after a long day.

Carry with you what you might need to make yourself comfortable. Such as snacks, lip balm, tissue, a nail file.

Don't feel you need to keep up. As long as you don't miss the boat or plane before it takes off, you need to experience the trip at the pace that works for you.

Be prepared to be uncomfortable at times. I don't like sticky sunscreen or insect repellant, but I will tolerate it so that I may experience the places that I want to see and enjoy.

Journal
If you travel, is there anything that works for you?

The HSP Tribe

It has been my extreme pleasure writing this book for you and all the other Highly Sensitive People out there in our world.

It is my greatest wish and prayer that all HSPs truly understand what a marvelous gift you are to the world, and that you will be brave enough to step into authentic presence and be the light for others to see.

Know that you are not alone. Yes, each of you is unique yet we are similar enough in nature to be a tribe of souls that see, feel, and love deeply.
The world needs us.

God Bless.

Johnnie Urban

P.S. Remember, to receive your complimentary companion workbook **40 Days To Fulfillment** link, email your book purchase receipt to; info@wonderfullifelearning.com
Subject line: workbook

Sources

SUGGESTED READING

The Highly Sensitive Person by Elaine Aron

The Highly Sensitive Person's Survival Guide by Ted Zeff, PhD.

The Power of Sensitivity by Ted Zeff, PhD.

Jeffrey E. Young, founder of Self-Sacrifice Schema

Jesus Calling by Sarah Young

Pain Free by Pete Egoscue

COACHING AND LIVE EVENT SUPPORT

Wonderful Life Learning
Johnnie Marie Urban, Founder and CEO
714-403-9256
www.WonderfulLifeLearning.com
info@WonderfulLifeLearning.com

Anthony Robbins Companies
TonyRobbins.com
RobbinsMadanesTraining.com

HEALTH AND WELLNESS

Netflix movies — *OMG GMO*

DR. Corey King
Tustin Chronic Condition Center
1076 E. First St. Ste. B
Tustin, CA 92780

Float Spot
http://floatspot.com/

Egoscue Pain Free Centers
www.Egoscue.com

Chris Kussoff
Exercise Therapist
27071 Cabot Rd. #107
Laguna Hills, Ca. 92653
949-716-7817
chris@egoscue.com

NUTRITIONAL SUPPORT & SUPPLEMENTS

Anti-Aging

NeriumAD™
http://jmurban.nerium.com
jmupartners@gmail.com

USANA
http://ThrivingWith.Usana.com